ASSAULT IN NORWAY

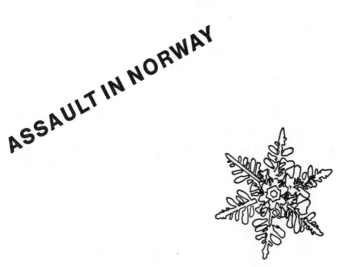

OTHER BOOKS BY THOMAS GALLAGHER

Nonfiction

Fire at Sea: The Story of the *Morro Castle*

The Doctors' Story

The X-Craft Raid

Novels

The Gathering Darkness

The Monogamist

Oona O'

ASSAULT IN NORWAY
SABOTAGING THE NAZI
NUCLEAR BOMB

Thomas Gallagher

HARCOURT BRACE JOVANOVICH
NEW YORK AND LONDON

Printed in the United States of America

Library of Congress Cataloging in Publication Data

Gallagher, Thomas Michael, date
　Assault in Norway.

　Includes Index.
　1. World War, 1939-1945—Secret service—Great
Britain.　2. Great Britain. Special Operations Executive.
3. Sabotage—Norway.　4. Atomic bomb.
I. Title.
D810.S7G26　　940.54′86′42　　74-20958
ISBN 0-15-109582-5

First edition

B C D E

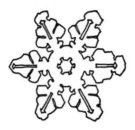

TO MY FRIEND
WILLIAM JOVANOVICH

"In the course of the last four months it has been made probable — through the work of [Frédéric] Joliot in France as well as [Enrico] Fermi and [Leo] Szilard in America — that it may become possible to set up a nuclear chain reaction in a large mass of uranium, by which vast amounts of power and large quantities of new radium-like elements would be generated. Now it appears almost certain that this could be achieved in the immediate future.

"This new phenomenon would also lead to the construction of bombs, and it is conceivable — though much less certain — that extremely powerful bombs of a new type may thus be constructed. A single bomb of this type, carried by boat and exploded in a port, might very well destroy the whole port together with some of the surrounding territory. However, such bombs might very well prove to be too heavy for transportation by air." Thus wrote Albert Einstein to President Franklin D. Roosevelt on August 2, 1939.

This is the first reference to the atomic bomb on record, and during the next two years its meaning and significance reverberated throughout scientific circles in Britain and the United States. Nuclear physicists realized clearly the implications of such a weapon, and many of them secretly hoped that it would be too difficult to achieve during World War II. In 1942 and 1943, when they realized that the construction of an atomic bomb was not only possible, but highly probable, their concern turned to alarm. The universal acceptance of German superiority in nuclear physics, coupled with the fear of what would happen if such destructive power was put at Hitler's disposal, drove them almost to panic. They knew, ignorant though they were at the time of Auschwitz,

Buchenwald, and Dachau, that Hitler would use it—against Britain and eventually the United States—until every democracy in the Western World became a police state under Nazi rule.

While Allied scientists worked frantically to catch up with Germany in the nuclear race, a secret mission was planned to destroy Germany's nuclear capacity. This book is devoted to that mission—to the volunteers, to their training, and to an appreciation of why their chance of success was so slim.

The story deserved to be based completely on original sources, especially on direct interviews with those who took part in the mission, and on their memoirs and diaries. I started my research, therefore, in August of 1972, in London, where the mission was planned and perfected under the direction of Special Operations Executive, a secret sabotage organization set up during World War II by authority of the British War Office. From London, after obtaining copies of operation plans and reports and official monographs on the mission from the Imperial War Museum, the Public Records Office, and Her Majesty's Stationery Office, I visited and interviewed, in Princess Risborough, Major-General Sir Colin Gubbins, the head of SOE during the war. Gubbins kindly offered me invaluable information on the inner workings of SOE in general, and on this secret mission in particular. From Gubbins's charming country home, I traveled a few days later to East Fairleigh, Kent, where, in another charming home, my hostess was Miss Margaret Wilson, the daughter of the late Colonel John S. Wilson, who headed the Norwegian Section of SOE during the war. Wilson had written extensively on the sabotage operations carried out in occupied Norway under his direction, and since no other Norwegian sabotage operation compared in importance with the one to which this book is devoted, I deeply appreciated Miss Wilson's kindness in offering me copies of everything her father had written on the subject.

Later, after talking in London with Sir Michael Perrin, deputy director of Britain's Atomic Project during World War II, I flew to Oslo, to interview the Norwegian volunteers who had carried out the mission. Claus Helberg, a sergeant in the Royal Norwegian Army at the time of the operation, was the first man I met. Besides giving me hours of his time during an interview in his Oslo office, he presented me with a long memoir he had written on the mission, and fully answered all the long queries I wrote him the following year after I returned to the United States. Arne Kjelstrup, another member of the original sabotage team, was equally kind and helpful when I spent several hours with him and his wife and son in their home in the suburbs of Oslo.

In Kongsberg, while on my way from Oslo to Rjukan and Vemork, where the sabotage action took place, I was helped immeasurably by Jens Poulsson, now a colonel in the Royal Norwegian Army, who had led the mission's advance party and had taken an active part, as had Helberg and Kjelstrup, in the sabotage itself. Poulsson supplied me not only with maps, his own memoirs and operation reports, but also with the kind of details and anecdotes that seem to come to mind only during an informal and relaxed interview. We met several times, at his office, for dinner, and at the Kongsberg railroad station.

After visiting the Vemork heavy-water plant, where the action took place, and talking with engineers and workers who were in and around the plant when the saboteurs arrived, I traveled north to the University of Trondheim to interview Dr. Jomar Brun, a former manager of the plant. He proved to be of invaluable help, supplying diagrams and photographs of the plant, explaining how he transmitted vital intelligence to SOE in London, and giving me a copy of his own written account of how he and his wife escaped to Sweden and eventually to Britain before the sabotage attack was launched. In Trondheim, I also met and interviewed Fredrik Bachke, the secret agent who delivered to Dr. and Mrs. Brun their escape orders, issued by General Hansteen of the Royal Norwegian Army.

From Trondheim I flew to Ålesund, where the man who led the sabotage party, Joachim Rönneberg, is today a broadcasting station executive. Having already spoken to several members of the sabotage mission, I had a long list of questions for Rönneberg. But when he started to speak, in his office in the broadcasting studio, I soon realized that my questions were superfluous. With what seemed total recall, he described the mission with such thoroughness and in such detail that I could not write fast enough. He also gave me a copy of his official operation report, which I found almost as valuable as the interview itself.

Back in Oslo, I had a long talk with Kjell Nielsen, a Vemork engineer who played an integral role in the mission as a member of the Norwegian underground. Like Rönneberg and Brun, Nielsen offered detailed information, and was kind enough to help me get in touch with another underground participant, Rolf Sörlie, who gave me a copy of his written account of the part he played before and after the attack. My Norwegian interpreter, Lars Loberg, had meanwhile obtained another written account, this one from Knut Lier-Hansen, an intrepid saboteur who played a vital role in the story's completely unexpected, unpredictable, and utterly hair-raising finale—an event that in fiction might be dismissed as excessive fantasy but that in this case happens to be authenticated truth.

Before leaving Norway I flew to Bergen to interview Fredrik Kayser, one of the three living saboteurs who were present in the plant's high-concentration room when the bombs were placed. His report not only corroborated everything Rönneberg had told me, but added his personal insights as well, things that he alone had experienced during those tense minutes before all hell broke loose.

Back in the United States, I obtained official documents from the National Archives in Washington, D.C., before traveling to Toronto to interview the "one-man advance party," as he was called, the first man to parachute into Norway before the mission, Einar Skinnarland, whose help, co-operation, and kindness I still deeply appreciate. Skinnarland gave me the decoded messages he had sent to and received from London in 1943; he also underscored for me, for the first time, the important contributions made by Norwegian farmers and reindeer herdsmen against the Germans occupying their country.

In Oakdale, Canada, I interviewed Jan Reimers, who acted as liaison between British and Norwegian intelligence agencies in London during the war. An astute man with a keen mind, Reimers seemed to know everything there is to know about how intelligence is gathered and used during a war. Finally, in Montreal, I spent an afternoon with Mrs. Sven Hurum (Gerd Vold), who in London during the war acted as secretary to the late Professor Leif Tronstad, the man who more than any other was the architect of this mission. Mrs. Hurum offered me anecdotes and details that only a woman would think of, and many are incorporated in this book, as are facts, direct quotes, and ideas gleaned from the material I was given.

It would be impossible for me to include the names of everyone I met and was helped by during my research, but among those who made important contributions to the mission and those whose generous assistance made my many months of research fruitful, I would like to mention the following people.

In Norway: Fredrik Bachke, Jomar Brun, Claus Helberg, Fredrik Kayser, Arne Kjelstrup, Knut Lier-Hansen, Lars Loberg, Ivar Nass, Kjell Nielsen, Astrid Øverbye, Wenja Paaske, Jens Anton Poulsson, Joachim H. Rönneberg, Halvor Röysland, Harald Selas, Torstein Skinnarland, Rolf Sörlie, Birger Strömsheim, Mrs. Leif Tronstad, Thor Viten.

In Britain: Major-General Sir Colin Gubbins, Anthony Land, Patricia Myers, Sir Michael W. Perrin, Michael Randolph, Margaret Wilson.

In Canada: Mrs. Sven Hurum, Jan H. Reimers, Einar Skinnarland.

In the United States: Alicia Boyd, Samuel A. Goudsmit, Walter Hunt, John D. Knowlton, Walter B. Mahony, Jr., Edward J. Reese.

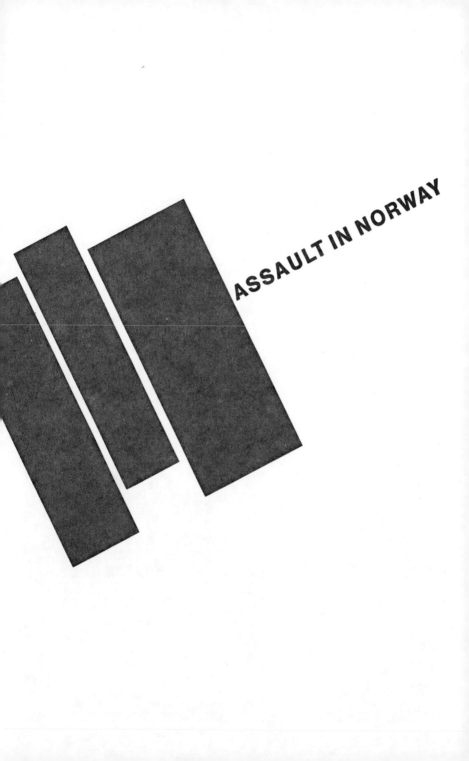

ASSAULT IN NORWAY

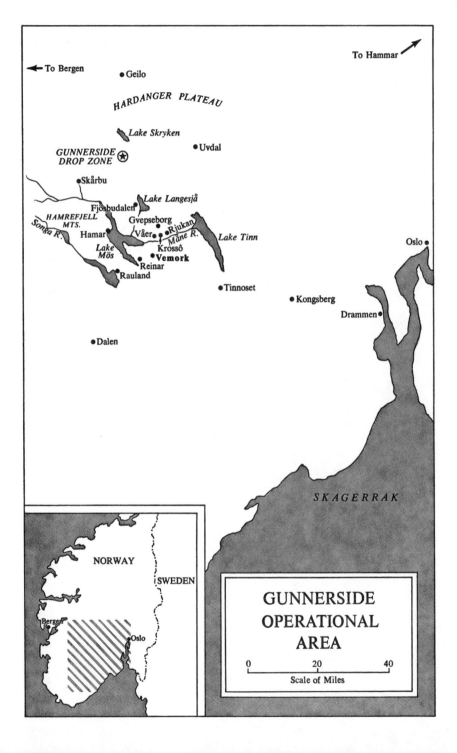

1 On the night of June 17, 1942, Winston Churchill boarded a Boeing flying boat and left Britain on what in retrospect may have been the most important mission of World War II. His final destination was Hyde Park, New York, where he was to meet with President Franklin Roosevelt in an effort to reach final decisions on Allied operations for 1942–43.

"Another matter lay heavy on my mind," Churchill wrote in *The Hinge of Fate*. "It was the question of 'Tube Alloys,' which was our code-word for what afterward became the atomic bomb."

British research and experiments had reached the point where definite agreements about nuclear energy had to be made with the United States, and it was felt that this could be achieved only by personal discussions between Churchill and the President. It had by then become widely known among the world's foremost physicists that the release of energy by atomic fission was possible, and that if such fission was achieved on a large scale, under ideal conditions, a nuclear weapon that could be used decisively in combat might be possible. Indeed, in America, all nonmilitary uranium research had already been stopped to enable effort to be concentrated on the manufacture of just such a weapon.

The urgency of the Churchill-Roosevelt meeting was underscored by the fact that in Germany, in December of 1938, an original experiment under the direction of the German physicist Otto Hahn had led to the discovery of atomic fission. This made a self-sustained, chain-reacting uranium pile at least a theoretical possibility, and it was known that the Germans had continued their experiments. Within a few months, physicists throughout the world were informing their respective governments that Hahn's discovery might lead to an unprecedented production of power and to superexplosives. Then in 1939 had come more ominous news: Germany had suddenly stopped all exports of uranium ore from Nazi-occupied Czechoslovakia.

But how close Germany was to constructing an atomic bomb was unknown to British and American physicists, and what little they did know they invariably interpreted in Germany's favor. Unless and until Allied intelligence uncovered proof to the contrary, it had to be assumed that the foremost German physicists and engineers were working on atomic research with the complete support and co-operation of their government and the industry under its control. Allied reconnaissance planes had brought back pictures of mysterious installations along the coast of France; intelligence data had been gathered on Germany's V-1 and V-2 rockets; and Hitler had boasted of secret weapons. What final use could the rockets have except to carry atomic explosives?

All the same, the Allies knew almost nothing about the German uranium project, and as one American atomic physicist, Samuel A. Goudsmit, put it, in his book *Alsos:* "Ordinary intelligence information yielded nothing of value. There were always fantastic rumors floating around about terrifying secret weapons and atomic bombs which were duly reported by the O.S.S. and British agents, but invariably the technical details were hopelessly nonsensical. The reason was obvious. No ordinary spy could get us the information we wanted for the simple reason that he lacked the scientific training to know what was essential. Only scientifically qualified personnel could get us that, and a Mata Hari with a Ph.D. in physics is rare, even in detective fiction."

On the other hand, Goudsmit was the first to agree with the U.S. military that "as a spy a qualified scientist would be a washout. He would in all likelihood give away more secrets than he could collect. It takes more than a false beard and forged papers to keep a scientist from identifying himself to other scientists, even if he can keep his mouth shut, which is unlikely where his specialty is concerned. Not that he will give away secrets deliberately. I have been present at discussions where two men were not supposed to exchange certain pieces of information. They did their level best to keep mum and discuss only what they were allowed to. But their very silences or denials on certain topics gave away everything to the rest of us present."

Churchill and Roosevelt had many other pressing problems to discuss in their June 1942 meeting. The great desert battles against Rommel's Panzer divisions were raging in North Africa. The United States Navy had not recovered from the near mortal blow it had suffered at Pearl Harbor. German U-boats were threatening ships carrying Lend-Lease war supplies to Britain and Russia. France had fallen, and much of London had been devastated. Plans for the great Normandy invasion were on the drawing board. But at the heart of all other considerations was the burning twofold question: How far ahead of the Allies were the Germans in nuclear research and what could be done to close the gap?

Churchill liked the spacious fuselage of the Boeing flying boat, and had enough confidence in chief pilot Captain Kelly Rogers to put in a special request that Rogers be in charge during the flight to the United States. The plane left the waters off Stranraer, Scotland, on the night of June 17, 1942, shortly before midnight. The moon was full, so Churchill sat for more than two hours in the copilot's seat, looking at the shining sea and thinking of the anxious situation in North Africa. Later, he slept well in what was called the "bridal suite" until, in broad daylight, they reached Newfoundland. Traveling with the sun had slowed the passage of time; they had had two luncheons, with a six-hour interval, and planned to have a late dinner after arrival in Washington, their first stop.

"For the last two hours we flew over the land," Churchill wrote, in commenting on the trip, "and it was about seven o'clock [in the evening] by American time when we approached Washington. As we gradually descended towards the Potomac River I noticed that the top of the Washington Monument, which is over five hundred and fifty feet high, was about our level, and I impressed upon Captain Kelly Rogers that it would be peculiarly unfortunate if we brought our story to an end by hitting this of all other objects in the world. He assured me that he would take special care to miss it. Thus we landed safely and smoothly on the Potomac after a journey of twenty-eight flying hours. . . . I repaired to the British Embassy for dinner. It was too late for me to fly on to Hyde Park that night. . . ."

Early the next morning, June 19, Churchill flew in a U.S. Army plane to Hyde Park, where he was greeted with "greatest cordiality" and driven all over the Roosevelt family estate by the President.

"In this drive I had some thoughtful moments," wrote Churchill. "Mr. Roosevelt's infirmity prevented him from using his feet on the brake, clutch, or accelerator. An ingenious arrangement enabled him to do everything with his arms, which were amazingly strong and muscular. He invited me to feel his biceps, saying that a famous prize-fighter had envied them. This was reassuring; but I confess that when on several occasions the car poised and backed on the grass verges of the precipices over the Hudson I hoped the mechanical devices and brakes would show no defects. All the time we talked business, and though I was careful not to take his attention off the driving we made more progress than we might have done in formal conference."

The next day, in what Churchill described as "a tiny little room which juts out on the ground floor" of the Roosevelt family home, "the most complex, and, as it proved, overwhelmingly the most important" subject—the atomic bomb—came up for discussion. Just three days before, Roosevelt had received a detailed report from Dr. Vannevar Bush, Director of the Office of Scientific Research and Development, on the status of the atomic-energy project in the United States. In his report Bush stated that it was possible to make a nuclear weapon that could be ready in time to influence the outcome of the war against the German Reich. The Germans were believed to be ahead of both the United States and Britain, and it was considered vital that they should not be the first to bring atomic weapons into the field of battle.

Churchill was likewise armed with the latest data on nuclear research, passed on to him by Lord Cherwell, his scientific adviser. "A great deal of work has been done both here and in America, and probably in Germany, on this super-explosive," Cherwell said in his report, "and it looks as if bombs might be produced and brought into use within, say, two years."

According to Lord Cherwell, one airplane would be able to carry one elaborate atomic bomb, weighing about a ton, that could explode with a force equal to about 2,000 tons of TNT. "People who are working on these problems consider the odds are ten to one on success within two years," he went on. "I would not bet more than two to one against, or even money. But I am quite clear we must go forward. It would be unforgivable if we let the Germans develop a process ahead of us by means of which they could defeat us or reverse the verdict after they had been defeated."

Although Churchill was "quite content with the existing explosives," he felt that he "must not stand in the path of improvement." On this, he and Roosevelt were in complete agreement.

"We both felt painfully the dangers of doing nothing," Churchill later wrote. "We knew what efforts the Germans were making to procure supplies of 'heavy water' — a sinister term, eerie, unnatural, which began to creep into our secret papers. What if the enemy should get an atomic bomb before we did! However sceptical one might feel about the assertions of scientists, much disputed among themselves and expressed in jargon incomprehensible to laymen, we could not run the mortal risk of being outstripped in this awful sphere."

To physicists everywhere, "heavy water" was not so much a sinister term as a substance used in nuclear research. Its importance to Britain, the United States, and Nazi Germany lay in the fact that it was known to be an exceptionally efficient moderator for slowing down neutrons in a uranium pile. By thus slowing down, without capturing, the neutrons produced by fission, the heavy water would, it was believed, enable the neutrons to collide with and split up uranium 235 atoms in the pile. This in turn would give rise to more neutrons, which would explode more atoms, until the reaction would sustain itself. It was this that would make possible an atomic bomb.

Heavy water is indistinguishable in appearance and chemical behavior from ordinary water, but, because it contains hydrogen atoms of double the atomic weight, it is about ten per cent heavier. In heavy water, that is, the hydrogen atoms consist of deuterium, the hydrogen isotope that has in its nucleus one proton and one neutron instead of one proton only. Heavy water is found in minute quantities in ordinary water, from which it is extremely difficult, time-consuming, and costly to separate. Only one hydro-electric plant in the world was capable at that time of manufacturing heavy water in significant quantities, and that plant was the Norsk Hydro Hydrogen Electrolysis plant at Vemork, Norway, a country occupied by the Germans since 1940.

Churchill and Roosevelt were also acutely aware of Allied intelligence reports from agents in Norway that Germany had twice ordered Norsk Hydro to increase its production of heavy water. In May 1940, immediately following the fall of Norway, Germany had ordered Norsk Hydro to increase its heavy-water production to 3,000 pounds a year. In February 1942, it was learned that Germany had demanded a further increase to 10,000 pounds a year. Since the Nazis had already placed an embargo on the export of uranium ore from Czechoslovakia, and since American and British physicists were in agreement that, given a large enough pile of uranium imbedded in a sufficient amount of heavy water, a self-sustained, chain-reacting pile could be made to operate, Churchill and Roosevelt had no choice but to assume that they and Hitler were in a race for possession of a weapon powerful enough to determine the fate of the free world.

In general terms, Churchill and Roosevelt agreed that Britain and the United States should pool their information and concentrate the work of British and American scientists in the United States and Canada. Since a large supply of heavy water was unavailable, the United States would start with a uranium-graphite pile, using graphite as the moderator, instead of a uranium–heavy-water pile. Meanwhile, a heavy-water plant was to be built in British Columbia on the chance that the use of graphite as a moderator proved to be impossible.

In the United States, the whole atomic-bomb program, called the "Manhattan Project," was put under the direction of General Leslie R. Groves, a blunt, forceful, and dedicated man who knew from the start that it was full of unknowns. "Nor was the full magnitude of the project generally appreciated," he later observed. "No one thought of it as entailing expenditures running into the billions of dollars. Not until later would it be recognized that chances would be taken that in more normal times would be considered reckless in the extreme. Not until later would it become accepted practice to proceed vigorously on major phases of the work despite large gaps in basic knowledge. Not until later would every other consideration, whether the advancement of knowledge for the sake of knowledge or the maintenance of friendly diplomatic relations with other powers, be subordinated to achieving the project's single overriding aim. Not until later would all concerned grow accustomed to the idea that, while normally haste makes waste, in this case haste was essential."

But if haste and the taking of risks and the expenditure of billions of dollars were essential to the Allies' project, so were they to the sabotaging or slowing down of Germany's. Somehow Germany's supposed two-year lead in nuclear research had to be offset. Crucial to that research was Germany's supply of heavy water, the most preferable substance to mix with uranium to obtain a chain-reacting pile. Crucial to the Allies' survival, therefore, was the cutting off of that supply at its source, the Norsk Hydro plant at Vemork, Norway. Only by doing so would they regain the time lost in the race with Germany for the bomb itself.

2 Many loyal Norwegians fled to Britain after the German occupation of their country in 1940, some immediately, in small steamers, trawlers, and sailboats, and others later, by way of Sweden and other, more circuitous, routes. Among those who fled later, probably the most important was Professor Leif Tronstad, of the Norwegian Institute of Technology in Trondheim. It was he who had planned, designed, and supervised the construction of the Vemork heavy-water plant.

Tronstad, a quick-witted, slender, short-waisted man with long legs, was also a long-distance runner, and loved exercise and action as much as he did science. He became a secret agent after the German occupation of his country and sent a steady flow of industrial information from his base at the institute in Trondheim to British and Norwegian authorities in Great Britain. It was from his friend Jomar Brun, the chief manager of the Vemork plant, that he learned of Germany's burning interest in the plant's production of heavy water, and it was from Tronstad that London first learned of it.

A copy of one of his many reports was read in London by Commander Eric Welch, head of Britain's Secret Intelligence Service. Welch asked a scientist attached to his office, "What in heaven's name is this stuff called 'heavy water'?"

As soon as the scientist explained the grave implications of Tronstad's report, Welch dispatched a return message asking for detailed information on Norsk Hydro's present production, its expansion plans, and its expected maximum capacity in future. A few days later he was shocked and puzzled when Tronstad, a Norwegian first and a spy second, not only refused the information, but also wanted to know whether Imperial Chemical Industries—

a British competitor of Norsk Hydro in peacetime—was behind the inquiry. "Remember," Tronstad added in his reply, "blood is thicker even than heavy water."

A few months later, in September 1941, after Tronstad learned through a double agent that the Germans were closing in on his illegal activities, he was forced to leave Norway. A devoted family man, he found it almost impossible to say good-by to his wife and children, but there was no choice. He had to get to Sweden without delay, and the sudden departure of an entire family would arouse too many suspicions.

The following month, he landed in England, and one of the first men he met was Commander Welch, who recalled with relish and delight the Trondheim radio message about blood being thicker than heavy water. It soon became apparent to Welch and others how important Tronstad was to Allied objectives in Norway. He had intimate knowledge of the area around the plant, complete command of the English language, outstanding forensic ability, and the energy of a dynamo. In addition, he had already won his stripes for his intelligence work in Trondheim, and he was well known among both British and American scientists, the very men who were now intensely occupied in war research. Most important of all, his friend and colleague Dr. Jomar Brun, the scientist who had collaborated with him during the planning and building of the heavy-water plant that now loomed so large in the race for an atomic bomb, was still at the plant, the chief manager in charge of production. Brun would know everything there was to know about the production of heavy water at Vemork; he would also be more than willing to pass the information on to London.

Tronstad became head of Section IV of the Norwegian High Command in London, in charge of intelligence, espionage, and sabotage, several months before Churchill's historic meeting with Roosevelt at Hyde Park. Much of Churchill's concern about Germany's efforts to procure supplies of heavy water—that "sinister term," as Churchill called it—was based on information obtained by Tronstad from Brun.

The British at this time had two separate and distinct organizations dealing with secret operations: the SIS (Secret Intelligence Service), under Commander Eric Welch, of the Naval Intelligence Department, and the SOE (Special Operations Executive), under Lord Selborne and Major-General Colin Gubbins, of the Ministry of Economic Warfare. The SIS trained agents in pure intelligence gathering and sent them back to Europe, where they obtained jobs and became accepted members of society. The SOE trained agents for sabotage operations to be carried out in Europe.

The SIS agents operated under the dictum that nothing should jeopardize their safe existence in Europe, and thus their ability to send an uninterrupted flow of vital information about German warships, U-boats, and troop movements. They were, for example, under strict instructions to make their messages to London as short as possible, to prevent the Germans from tracking the various locations of their sending sets. As a result, the agents sometimes made the messages recondite to the point of incomprehensibility. "What the hell does he mean?" the man receiving the message in London would often ask himself. It was like someone sending a telegram, trying desperately to save money by saying as much as possible in as few words as possible.

These agents, trained as they were in the art of staying safely ensconced in the society in which they operated, were unhappy about SOE agents—the men of action—going into large ports like Bergen to sabotage small merchant ships or dock installations. Such actions invariably increased Gestapo activity in those areas and, as a result, threatened what SIS agents considered their much more vital intelligence gathering.

One of Leif Tronstad's great contributions to the Allied war effort was his ability to bridge the gap between the operational and the pure-intelligence agents working in Norway. He got along as well with Colonel John S. ("Jack") Wilson, head of the Norwegian Section of SOE, as he did with Commander Welch, of SIS. He was, in fact, considered one of Norway's best ambassadors during the war, and his arrival in Britain, in October 1941, could not have been better timed. The Vemork heavy-water plant had to be sabotaged, at all costs, by SOE's operational agents, and information about the plant had to be gathered, at all costs, by SIS's pure-intelligence agents. Both kinds of agents were needed, and neither was more vital than the other, at least as far as this operation was concerned. No one knew this better than Tronstad, an intellectual who could evaluate within minutes all the technical details sent in by the intelligence-gathering agents in Norway, and a sportsman who delighted in taking an active part in the sabotage and parachute-jumping exercises of those being trained for duty as operational agents.

The problem was how to destroy Vemork's capacity for making heavy water. The high-concentration room was situated in the basement of a stone, steel, and concrete building that stood like an eagle's nest on a cliffside in a mountain wilderness. It was an almost impossible target for night bombers, which was all that Britain had at the time, and a difficult target for a ground attack.

As efforts continued at the highest levels to solve the problem, the need for fresh information about the plant increased. Somehow a direct and dependable link had to be established between Norwegian agents working at the plant and living in the nearby town of Rjukan and those planning the attack in Britain.

In the middle of March 1942, the problem was solved by one of those odd coincidences that seem to happen so often in wartime, when time and events and the actions of men mesh, overlap, and sometimes collide. Six Norwegian patriots, among them SOE's leading agent in Norway, suddenly arrived in Aberdeen, Scotland, after seizing an old Norwegian coastal steamer and piloting it across the North Sea. One of these men was Einar Skinnarland, a powerful, barrel-chested man in his early twenties, with a ruddy face, blond hair, and the easy gait of a natural athlete. He looked, spoke, and acted like a loyal Norwegian, but was nevertheless sent to "Patriotic School," a security detention camp where everyone of whatever nationality arriving in Britain was carefully interrogated before being released into society.

"The man who questioned me was British," Skinnarland said later, "but he knew Norway as well as he did his own hand. It was the same if you were French or Polish. They had an expert to question you."

Skinnarland spoke English fluently, was a champion skier and a radio, or wireless, operator. He had had contact with the Signals Chief of the Central Leadership of the Military Organization of Resistance, or Milorg, in Oslo. Most important of all, he came from Rjukan, where his regular occupation was construction superintendent on the hydroelectric dam on Lake Mös, only a few miles to the west of Vemork, and he knew several technicians at the Vemork plant. As an expert skier, he also had an intimate knowledge of the surrounding mountain area and was on friendly terms with the farmers who somehow managed to survive in that desolate and lonely land. If anyone could provide clear, accurate communication between Vemork and London, it was Einar Skinnarland. And he was willing to be hurried through an SOE training course and be parachuted back into Norway as soon as possible. If he got back to his job in time (he had taken a short leave "to go on a skiing trip"), his absence would not be noted.

"Our juice is very important," Tronstad said in his first courier-delivered letter to Jomar Brun, in the spring of 1942, shortly after Skinnarland's return to Norway. "Our juice" was their term for heavy water. Tronstad, who signed his letters to Brun "Mikkel," the Norwegian word for fox, added that he wanted to be kept informed about the plant's production of heavy water, why the Germans were pressing for an increase in its production, and how fast it was being shipped to Germany.

In a later letter, expressing the extreme urgency of the heavy-water problem, Tronstad asked if Brun "could conceive a plan for transporting a considerable quantity of heavy water from Vemork to Britain." In his reply, Brun said that it would be almost impossible, that the only chance would be the landing of a British plane on a large frozen lake in the mountains near Vemork. He suggested Lake Såheimbotn, because it was long enough for a landing and was on the plant's side of the deep gorge cut by the Måne River. "If that could be realized," he added, "I might be able, with the aid of Norwegian compatriots, to transfer our juice from the plant to the plane."

That plan was abandoned, and while others were being discussed in London, Brun augmented his intelligence-gathering activities by moonlighting as an "operational agent." He began sabotaging the production of heavy water at the plant by "secretly adding castor oil to the electrolyte." This caused a heavy foaming in the heavy-water system, and though it did not destroy the heavy water, it did stop production for hours, and sometimes for days. The production increase the Germans expected after the plant's expansion from nine to eighteen high-concentration cells was therefore "very slight indeed," Brun said.

He did not know it at the time, but other Norwegians at the plant were adding cod-liver oil to the high-concentration containers. At times there was so much frothing and foaming in the heavy-water system that Brun himself, to avert suspicion, "had to recommend some device to suppress it somewhat." However, the frothing continued as long as he was there.

Brun also obtained photographs, drawings, and minute details of the plant. He had these microphotographed by a trusted friend in Rjukan, then concealed the microphotographs in toothpaste tubes for delivery by courier through Sweden to Tronstad in London.

Churchill was briefed on all this crucial intelligence before his meeting with Roosevelt in June 1942, and it was on his return to

Britain that the Norsk Hydro plant at Vemork became a top-priority sabotage target. In July, the British War Cabinet approached Combined Operations Command with an urgent request that Vemork be attacked with sufficient force to destroy all accumulated stocks of heavy water, the major pieces of machinery in the electrolysis plant used for its production, and the power station situated at the rear of the plant.

The urgency of the request was reflected in the extremely hazardous plan proposed. Thirty-four commandos of the First Airborne Division were to be transported in two Horsa gliders, each towed by a Halifax bomber, across the North Sea to Hardanger Plateau, a vast and desolate mountain area to the northwest of the Rjukan-Vemork area. There the towlines were to be let go, and the gliders, laden with troops, demolition equipment, guns, and folding bicycles, were to glide silently down through the moonlight for a soft landing on the marshy edge of Lake Mös, the largest of the plateau's lakes, whose waters fed the Vemork plant's turbines.

The first party to land was to wait up to half an hour for the second; if the second party did not appear, it was to proceed independently—downhill in the darkness, on bicycles, along a mountain road toward the target on the north side of the gorge. When they reached the suspension bridge leading across the gorge to the plant, they were to kill, as quietly as possible, the German guards on the bridge, enter the plant, and destroy, in order of priority, the machinery and the existing stocks of heavy water. The force was then to split up into small groups of not more than three men and make its way to Sweden. Anyone wounded was to be given an injection of morphine and left at the side of the road, after all maps, except the small-scale map covering the whole country, were removed from him. The high-concentration heavy water was stored in small (200 cubic-centimeter) steel flasks, and a few of these were to be brought back if possible.

An advance party of four Norwegians was to be flown from Britain and dropped by parachute several weeks before the attack, to reconnoiter for all possible knowledge of the layout, the likely opposition, the routes to and from the target, and the guards, both German and Norwegian, to be expected along the way. The advance party was also to provide weather reports for the November moon period selected for the attack; operate Eureka, a navigational aid, to guide the aircraft on the night of the operation; light up the landing site with beacons; cut all telephone wires in the vicinity immediately before the landing, and guide the troops to the target area.

Security was considered extremely important, since any intelligence leak would not only jeopardize the lives of the thirty-four men involved, but also prevent a follow-up attack should this one fail. A carefully conceived cover story was put out about a contest between the British Army Engineers and a similar company of U.S. Army Engineers for a mythical "Washington Cup." The competition was said to involve a long approach by either glider or parachute, followed by a complicated demolition task, and conclude with a strenuous endurance test. Under this cover story the whole of the training, the movements, and the demands for stores and equipment were to be made to avoid arousing suspicion. The competition for the Washington Cup was to be talked about openly, so that anyone who had contact with the force—the cooks, the quartermasters, the workshop personnel—would be fully convinced by the story.

When Combined Operations turned to SOE for advice, the Norwegian Section objected to the plan on the grounds that it was ill-conceived and susceptible to too many failures at too many stages in its operation. Wilson and Tronstad pointed out the following:

1. Of all countries, Norway is the least suitable for glider operations. Its landing grounds are few; its mountains thickly clustered, precipitous, and angry. The broken countryside, made up of a conglomerate of lakes, hills, bogs, boulders, marshes, and moors, throws up air pockets and atmospheric currents.

2. The 400-mile glider tow proposed was far longer than any ever attempted, even in daylight.

3. The success of the operation demanded exceptionally favorable weather conditions on Hardanger Plateau, where in winter the weather was seldom favorable and hardly ever predictable.

4. The plateau is noted for sudden up-and-down air currents powerful enough to make a bucking bronco of a Horsa glider.

5. The landing site would be difficult to identify if clouds obscured the moon, or if, more likely at that altitude, there was a low cloud cover.

6. The night landing of a fragile craft in an area known for its fissures and ridges, huge boulders, and outcrops of rock would be extremely hazardous.

7. Though many of the lakes on Hardanger Plateau are frozen in November, the ice would not yet be strong enough to bear the weight of a heavily laden Horsa glider.

8. The folding bicycles would prove to be worthless in the event of a snowfall, or if the mountain road leading to the Vemork plant turned out to be coated with ice, which in November might easily be the case.

9. After the attack, the saboteurs would have to make their way 400 miles to the Swedish border under winter conditions with which they were unfamiliar.

General Leslie Groves, meanwhile, insisted that the Vemork plant be either bombed from the air or sabotaged on the ground. And the British War Cabinet had given highest priority to the destruction of the plant's capacity to produce heavy water.

Tronstad vehemently opposed any idea of bombing the plant from the air. He pointed out that Rjukan, the electrical-power center of southern Norway, lies in a very deep valley, the thickly forested sides of which rise almost vertically from a narrow river bed to over 3,000 feet.

"The valley is so deep," he said, "that throughout the winter the sun's rays never reach Rjukan's streets. If stray bombs were to hit the liquid-ammonia storage tanks at the bottom of that valley, the whole Rjukan population would be in the gravest danger."

And so, Combined Operations, under pressure from both Washington and the British War Cabinet to get the job done, overruled SOE's objection to an attack by glider-borne troops and set in motion the wheels of "Freshman," the code name for the glider-towing operation.

3 Special Operations Executive already had an advance party of four Norwegians standing by for a favorable opportunity to parachute into Norway and set up a base camp on Hardanger Plateau for future sabotage operations. When these four men were put at the disposal of Combined Operations, they were sent to London from their training camp in Scotland to meet with Professor Tronstad and Colonel Wilson. All were experienced skiers and in excellent physical condition; all but one had grown up in Rjukan, knew the region intimately, and were familiar with local underground members.

Tronstad and Wilson met first, in private, with the leader of the group, Sub-Lieutenant Jens Anton Poulsson, a twenty-four-year-old with a tall, tennis player's figure and sharp features set in a face so lean that even his modest mustache looked bold. After listening to a short, almost laconic description of the operation, Poulsson said, "Interesting," and knocked dead ashes from his pipe into the palm of his hand. Tronstad and Wilson were soon to learn that Poulsson's pipe was as necessary a part of him as eyeglasses are to a man with weak eyes. Whether he was lighting it, stuffing it, smoking it, or cleaning it, he made it a friend and companion. Even in snapshots taken of him in Norway before the German occupation, the pipe was always present, cupped in his hand or sticking from his mouth, as essential to the composition of the picture as the mustache itself.

Born and raised in Rjukan, Poulsson had high stakes in the sabotage operation, for his parents, two sisters, and younger brother were still living in Rjukan, only two and a half miles from the Vemork plant. If he were captured and his identity discovered by the Germans, his entire family would undoubtedly be sent to the infamous concentration camp at Grini, in Norway.

Second in command was another Rjukan man, now in charge of the Resistance Museum in Oslo. Knut Haugland's neat, civil-servant appearance today belies the cliché picture of a resistance fighter. A radio operator on a merchantman before being mobilized in 1940, he joined the rear-guard action against the Germans' sixty-two-day invasion of Norway, and showed the same kind of courage, stamina, and spirit that he did after the war, in 1947, when he joined the crew of *Kon-Tiki* and took part in one of the most exciting and momentous voyages in the history of the sea. He was chosen for the Vemork mission not only because of his knowledge of the Rjukan area, but also because he supplied something essential—his experience as a wireless operator—to the success of the mission. He was an expert radioman, with knowl-edge of the latest British and American wireless sets, and he had all the different code systems at his finger ends.

Sergeant Claus Helberg, as a boy, had sat next to Poulsson at Rjukan's public school. Even then, Helberg had a habit of scratching the top of his head while ruminating, and now, as an adult, whenever his handsome face became thoughtful, he invol-untarily reached up to the top of his head as if to facilitate the movement of his train of thought. At school he was known for the ease with which he could get into and out of trouble, and nothing had happened since to alter that judgment of him. He was a daring improviser, with an innocent face; as his friends put it, the daring got him into trouble, the improvisation out of it.

The fourth man, Sergeant Arne Kjelstrup, was neither a Rjukan man nor as tall as the other three. But what he lacked in height he made up for in the breadth of his chest and the strength of his arms and broad, sloping shoulders. He was a plumber from Oslo, and before the war he had spent many winter weekends in the Rjukan region of Telemark, where competitive skiing was born.

Like all of SOE's secret operatives, Poulsson and his men had been trained in Scotland, at what the Germans called the "International Gangster School." There were three good reasons for this title: SOE was a vast organization divided into sections according to nationality; it carried on sabotage and espionage all over Europe; and its methods were, given the unprecedented ruthlessness of the enemy, gangsterlike. In the Norwegian Section of SOE, for example, Poulsson and his men, besides undergoing basic infantry training, learned how to force locks and break open safes, how to use fuses and detonators, and how to make their own booby traps. They learned how to handle TNT, dynamite, guncotton, and plastic explosive; how to use pistols, knives, chloroform, poison, and their own fists and feet. They practiced blowing holes in reinforced concrete walls and breaking down steel doors, and they knew what kind and what amount of explosive to use in each case. Because ammunition in the operational area would be limited and irreplaceable, they were taught not to keep the index finger pressed against the trigger of a Tommy gun. The point was to fire single shots, if possible, by touching the trigger and then quickly letting go, and they found that the best way to accomplish this was to shoot from the hip. They preferred shooting from the shoulder, but when they did, they always fired double shots. One day they were each allotted 200 shots, and by shooting single shots from the hip, eighty-five per cent of all their shots were hits.

At parachute training school, they were put through such exercises as jumping off high platforms with their knees bent, falling from lower platforms on their sides and rolling over, and being dragged by rope along the ground. Then came their first actual parachute jump, from a Halifax bomber flying at a height of about 1,500 feet.

"The scariest training exercise, though," Helberg recalled, "was jumping from a balloon in the dark. It was required of everyone at the school, and if you didn't jump, you didn't graduate."

A standard barrage balloon of the type used during the London blitz carried the jumpers into the air. It was equipped with a square platform suspended underneath, and in the middle of the platform was a round hole through which, as the balloon went higher and higher, the dim, miniature outlines of camouflaged army jeeps could be seen. Poulsson and his men and their instructor had to cling to the swaying platform's outer railing as they ascended, for fear of falling through the hole, and to make matters worse, they could hear the other instructors on the ground joking about the poor bastards who were going up to jump, while their own instructor shouted down comments of his own.

When it came time to jump, a check was made to be sure the men knew the order in which they were to drop through the hole. Then the instructor shouted "Go!" to the first man. After a pause, he shouted "Go!" to the second man. Then, once more, in exactly the same way, "Go!" to the third man. Then one final time before he went through the hole himself.

"It was not at all like jumping from a plane," Helberg has said. "When you jump from a plane, the wind takes you so fast horizontally that your chute opens right away—that is, in about a second and a half. But when you jump from a balloon, you fall straight down about 250 feet before anything happens. It takes about five seconds for the chute to open, and since you can't see how close you are to earth, you keep wondering, Will I hit before it opens? Everything is quiet; there is no horizontal wind, no roar from the plane's engine. It's dark, and as you fall you get this terrifying sense of the increasing velocity of your descent from the sound of the air rushing through your clothing. Then, when your chute finally does open, you still can't see the ground, but you can hear the instructors discussing the progress of the jumpers coming down. All in all, a spooky experience."

In London, when they each met with Tronstad and Wilson, Poulsson was the only one informed of the actual assignment.

"This was to avoid the risk of having information leak out that the Allies were planning an attack on the Vemork plant," Poulsson later explained. "The others thought we were going over to instruct the home forces in preparation for the eventual takeover of our country. I was to tell them the truth only after we parachuted into Norway and set up our base camp."

In all such top-secret missions, there are a highly select few who know everything about the planning, aims, logistics, risks, and personnel involved. Below these are a privileged few who know something but not everything. And below them are the others, who are allowed to know only the bits and pieces they have to know in order to function efficiently in the whole scheme of things. Tronstad and Wilson told Poulsson nothing about the grave significance of the heavy water produced at the Vemork plant, but they did want him to know that the mission, designed to thwart Germany's most ambitious war project, was of the utmost importance.

"The Germans could destroy all of London if they succeed," Wilson had said.

"I really didn't believe him," Poulsson said later. "In those days no one thought in terms of one bomb destroying a whole city. Not that he used the word 'bomb.' I didn't know what he meant. I just knew he would not have said what he did if the mission were not important."

After being issued pounds from the Bank of England, the four volunteers went shopping for all the necessary equipment: winter clothing, including ski boots and trousers, walking boots, windbreakers, gloves, mittens, balaclava helmets; tents, compasses, frostbite ointment, and sleeping bags. They went first to Lillywhites, the famous sporting-goods store in London, and, like tourists unaware that the whole world was at war, asked to see everything the store had in stock for winter sports. Lillywhites, accustomed to the idiosyncrasies of the British upper class, even in wartime, was not about to lose poise in the presence of tourists, but unfortunately the store's skis and ski boots were made for Alpine, or downhill, skiing, not for the kind of Nordic, or cross-country, skiing that Poulsson and his men would be doing in Norway. Nor were English sleeping bags equal to the sub-zero temperatures the four men would be subjected to if the glider mission failed and they were forced to spend the entire winter up on Hardanger Plateau. The sleeping bags had to be filled with down, and the stitching could not penetrate the area where the down was located. The inner part, that is, had to be divided into compartments, and each compartment had to be filled with down and stitched separately. At the same time, the inner layer of the bag had to be resistant to water, the outer layer capable of shedding water, and yet both layers had to breathe, too.

They finally found a bedding firm, just to the north of Trafalgar Square, where, when they explained their problem and said that money was no obstacle, they were listened to and then taken to the firm's factory. There the manager said he had never made a sleeping bag but suggested that he try a doll-sized model. He did, and after suggestions and alterations were made, production was started on full-sized bags. Other necessary items—rucksacks, gloves, and soft, sheepskin-lined white boots were made of British material at the Norwegian army supply workshop in Dumfries, Scotland. Nordic skis and ski boots were obtained from a Norwegian skiing-equipment company in Iceland, and also from the steady flow of Norwegians fleeing to Britain in fishing and sailing boats.

"We managed, after a good deal of effort, to get hold of all the equipment we needed," Helberg recalled later. "By the end of August we had everything packed and were ready to go. We just had to wait for a moonlit night and good flying weather. We didn't know it then, but from the moment we were packed and ready to go, and for six months after we landed, the weather was to be our foremost enemy."

Twice in September they shook hands with Tronstad and

Wilson at the airfield in Scotland and boarded a Halifax bomber. Twice they roared off into the night, sitting on their parachutes amongst parcels containing leaflets to be dropped on the return journey to conceal the plane's real mission. Twice they waited in tense, expectant silence, ghostly in their white camouflage ski outfits, as the plane approached Norway's coastline and the mountains and fjords beyond.

"On the first flight," according to Helberg, "one of the plane's engines burned up, and we barely made it back to Britain. On the second flight, we were forced to turn and go back because of a radio report that there would be dense fog over Britain later that night. We returned just in time to see the notorious English fog pour in, thick as a wall. Landing in that kind of fog is nearly impossible, and we just made it."

Finally, on October 18, with a full "bomber's moon" overhead, Poulsson and his men found themselves looking down from an altitude of 10,000 feet on Hardanger Plateau. Only a few hours earlier they had been loafing in the sun on a lawn by the sea in Scotland; now, as the plane continued on its eastward course, they began searching for the area where they were supposed to jump— the level, rockless marshes around Ugleflott. They had already passed Lake Totak—they all agreed on that—but where were they now? The plateau, 3,500 square miles of barren, virtually uninhabited territory, the largest and wildest mountain plateau in Europe, stretched out as far as their eyes could see, white and beautiful, a bewitching sight in the moonlight. Three thousand feet above sea level, with countless hills, rolling plains, brooks, rivers, lakes, moors, marshes, and mountains, it was something like a small Alaska. And yet it appeared so much more level from 10,000 feet than Poulsson and Helberg remembered it on skis. Was it really this flat in the southern part? If so, they would have only the lakes, still not solidly frozen, to worry about when they jumped.

As they waited, hoping the navigator would find Ugleflott,

the joy of returning to Norway was mingled with the excitement of the jump, with the mechanics of it, the laws of motion and gravity involved. Extending from each man's parachute was a long line, the end of which was fastened to a steel wire inside the plane. When he dropped through the hole into space, the line, sixteen feet long, would be pulled taut and begin drawing out the parachute. He did not have to do anything himself except drop through the hole and fall sixteen feet. From that point on, the line would open the parachute and then break, from his weight, as he descended.

The four volunteers were to go first; then the dispatcher was to drop twelve coffin-size metal containers of equipment, supplies, weapons, ammunition, and food through the hole after them. Each container had its own parachute, with a string attached to the same steel wire inside the plane.

Suddenly the plane's wings began to vibrate as the pilot pointed its nose downward and slowed the engines. When it reached an altitude of 1,000 feet and leveled off, the ground no longer looked flat and rockless. There were ridges, boulders, and hills everywhere, but the warning lamp in the ceiling of the plane turned to red anyway.

"Action stations!" the dispatcher shouted in a sharp, commanding voice that allowed no room for hesitation. It was important that the men jump in rapid succession, for the plane was traveling at a speed of about 180 feet a second. This meant that if the second man jumped ten seconds after the first man, he would find himself 600 yards away from the first man when he reached the ground. If the third and fourth man did the same thing—that is, hesitated ten seconds before jumping—the first and last man would be separated by over a mile. It was the dispatcher's responsibility to see that only a second separated one jump from another.

Poulsson, the first jumper, was already in position, with his legs dangling through the hole in the belly of the plane. The parachute was as bulky and unwieldy as a loaded rucksack, and yet he and it had to go through the hole cleanly to prevent fouling the lines and harness. He kept reminding himself of this as the wind grabbed and pulled at his dangling legs with the force of racing water. Far below were hills, ridges, lakes, and boulders, seemingly jumbled together, because of the speed of the plane and his restricted vision. Waiting two seconds is a long wait under such circumstances, and it took that long, but no longer, for the order to jump to come.

"Number one! Go!" the dispatcher shouted, and down through the hole went Poulsson.

"Haugland was the second to go, and Arne Kjelstrup the third," Helberg recalls. "The next second I, too, jumped out into the cold of the night. The wind tore and pulled at me as I fell, and the parachute was drawn open by the string. Suddenly the parachute filled with air and stiffened; there was a violent jerk as it opened wide above me. Two seconds and it was all over. The most important thing had happened. The parachute had opened without a hitch. I found myself floating slowly down toward the ground, with all our equipment, twelve huge containers, floating down through the moonlight behind us, and the plane disappearing westwards."

The pilot had circled and backtracked so the equipment would not be too far away from where they landed, but the navigator had not found Ugleflott after all. They landed on a mountainside strewn with the kind of boulders and rocks that break knees and legs and cut into flesh even in daylight landings. But they were all well-trained natural athletes, and they knew that, no matter what happened, the important thing was to get free of the parachute as quickly as possible after reaching the ground.

"Luckily, the crosswind was not too bad, so we all landed safely, and so did our containers," Helberg said. "Even our transmitter appeared to have survived the rough terrain rather well. And here we were, in Norway, cold and inhospitable, but marvelous all the same. After a year in Britain, we were of course not used to the sharp, dry cold of the plateau, let alone its snowy desolation and loneliness."

He sat there for a moment, the snow around his waist moving with the wind like sand. Gone was the green turf of Scotland, the rustle of leaves, and the sound of the sea. The snow looked bluish white in the moonlight against his gloved hand. He cupped some up and let the wind take it as he looked up at the absolutely clear dome of sky above him. Britain seemed so far away, and yet so near, like home, almost.

Since their containers of supplies and equipment were too scattered to be retrieved that night, they gathered together only the essentials, some food and their sleeping bags, and made camp behind a huge boulder that served as a windbreak.

When they were settled, Poulsson got out his pipe and began stuffing it with tobacco. Everyone watched in silence and with appreciation, for it was a calming sight to see. "It's time I told you the truth," he said as he struck a match and began puffing. "We were not sent over as instructors for the home forces. That was just a cover story. We're here on a far more vital assignment—to help destroy the heavy-water factory at Vemork. Two British gliders with thirty to forty Royal Engineers are to be towed in from Scotland. We're to find a good landing site for the gliders and then guide the troops from the landing site to Vemork. The British are not bringing skis with them, so the landing site must be close to some road, and not too far from Vemork."

Helberg was already scratching the top of his head, as if to speed up his train of thought. "The Skoland marshes," he said, "are four miles east of the Lake Mös dam. They're also fairly close to the Vemork plant, and they adjoin a road the British troops can use for their approach."

Poulsson puffed away and nodded, having had the same idea himself. "The operation is to be carried out in the next moon period," he went on. "So we have four weeks to reconnoiter the plant, get information on the German guards, and check on the landing site. But first thing tomorrow, before we do anything else, we have to get our equipment and supplies together. The dispatcher got us out of that plane pretty quickly, but I don't know about the containers. Some of them must be two miles from here."

"I just hope nothing happened to the one carrying our skis and ski poles," Kjelstrup said.

"Nothing happened to it," Poulsson said. "It's metal and very strong."

What did worry him, though, was the possibility of snow falling during the night. If that happened, they might never find the containers. He glanced up at the full moon and almost cloudless sky. It certainly did not look like snow, but on the plateau you could never tell.

"Good night," he said.

4

It took Poulsson and his men two full days of wallowing through a boundless sea of snow beneath a glittering sun to recover their supplies. Using their makeshift campsite as a starting point, each man went off in a different direction and came back an hour or two later either dragging a container or shaking his head in disgust. Sometimes one of them would clearly "see" a container a half mile off and start toward it, only to have it disappear in the deceptive whiteness while he was approaching it, or turn into something else entirely by the time he reached it. Even when he saw nothing in the direction in which he was walking, he had to continue for at least a mile on the chance that a container might be resting amongst the various small hills and hollows and creek beds here and there. Kjelstrup, his boots bringing up heavy loads of slush with each step, kept thinking of the skis and poles. They were in one of the last containers to be found.

"How easily we could have retrieved everything if we had found the skis and poles first!" he said.

Meanwhile, they learned from their maps that they had landed ten miles farther west than anticipated, at Fjarfeit, in the mountain range east of the Songa River. The distance from Fjarfeit to the Skoland marshes Poulsson figured to be about sixty-five miles. No great distance for expert skiers under ordinary skiing conditions, but they had to transport a four-week supply of food, sleeping bags, a transmitter with a storage battery and charging unit, a portable Eureka navigational aid, weapons, ammunition, tents, and equipment—altogether about 650 pounds.

Another blow was the discovery that the paraffin for their Primus stoves had been lost. With paraffin for cooking and warmth, they could have gone directly across the plateau in a straight line to the Skoland marshes. Now they would have to forgo that direct mountain route and move along the winding Songa valley, where birch was available for firewood and there were huts in which they could spend the nights. The longer and slower route would demand a greater consumption of food, though, and they had just enough to sustain them until the next full moon, when the gliders were scheduled to land.

"I hoped that our food, with the strictest rationing, would be sufficient for thirty days," Poulsson later said. "We had been told to make no outside contacts except in the gravest emergency, so we could not count on getting any extra flour or meat from the few farmers in the area. It was important that we avoid being seen by anyone."

On the third day, October 22, after they had gathered all their equipment, packed what they needed, and hidden the rest in a cache in the ground for recovery after completion of the operation, they began their march toward the marshes. At such high altitudes, the maximum load a skier can carry is about sixty-five pounds. Not counting what they had cached away, their supplies and equipment consisted of eight such loads. This meant that each man in their party of four had to cover the same distance three times: he had to carry his first load as far as he decided he could carry the second, then go back the same distance for the second and carry it back again to where he had left the first. Sometimes, depending upon how much daylight was left, they would make several short triple trips rather than two or three long ones.

For days they pushed their way along riverbanks stubbled with birch and covered with snow so wet that it clung in clumps to the bottom of their skis. Had the lakes, marshes, and rivers been frozen solid enough to ski on, the going would have been much easier. But winter had come late to Hardanger Plateau, and they had to cling to the shores and banks, where the ground was rugged and the snow heavy and deep. Even when they came to a lake or marsh that could be walked on here and there, the surface water on the ice soaked their feet, and sometimes they fell through and stood waist high in near-freezing water.

Counting the repeat trips they had to make for the second load, their actual advance on days when they ran into difficult terrain amounted to only a few miles. In addition, there was the wet, scrubby birch that they had to dutifully chop and split every evening, though it seldom burned long enough to dry their socks and clothing. The mere smell, sound, and sight of a fire helped, though, so they always made one after each day's grind. Watching the sparks fly off the wood, listening to the spit and crackle of the sap made them remember what Norway was like before the German occupation. Now and then they were lucky enough to come upon a cabin whose cupboard contained a can or two of food, and once, in an unoccupied summer farmhouse, they found not only flour, but meat as well. The meat was frozen as hard as a rock, but they chopped it into pieces with an ax, put the pieces in a pot half filled with snow water, and started a fire.

"We ate our fill for the first time since our arrival," Poulsson recalled. "There was dry firewood for a change, and we used what we needed to cook the meat and warm ourselves."

But as their cross-country trek continued and their food supply dwindled, malnutrition increased their fatigue and severely limited the distance they were able to cover in a single day. Poulsson developed a throbbing boil on his left hand and, when he wasn't skiing, had to put his arm in a sling. He and the others had kept themselves in excellent condition during the waiting period in Britain, but the grueling march on short rations sapped their strength.

"On one of the last days en route," Helberg remembered, "we only managed a distance, all told, of about three-quarters of a mile."

By then a man's daily ration was limited to one-quarter of a loaf of pemmican (dried meat pounded into a powder and mixed with fat and dried fruits and pressed into a loaf or into small cakes), a fistful of oatmeal, a fistful of flour, four biscuits, a table-spoon of butter, a little cheese, and a bit of chocolate.

"Fortunately, there were many cabins in the valleys, so we didn't have to sleep outdoors," Helberg added. "Had we been forced to spend the nights out in the open, on top of all the other hardships, I don't see how we could have made it."

On October 30, twelve days after the parachute landing, they came to another empty cabin, at Reinar, about seven miles south of their objective—the Skoland marshes around Lake Mös. There they found no food, but enough wood to keep them warm. Only two weeks remained before the scheduled glider landing, and they still had to contact London, reconnoiter the target area, inspect the proposed landing site, and somehow obtain more food. As Knut Haugland prepared to set up an antenna for his sending set, Helberg volunteered to ski back to the unoccupied summer farm and steal as much food as he could carry. The trip both ways totaled fifty miles, through snow as soft and wet as sherbet, but he would be carrying only one load back this time, not two.

At the same time, Poulsson and Kjelstrup would inspect the landing site. Haugland would remain behind in the cabin and get in touch with London. They would rendezvous at the cabin in three days.

"Kjelstrup and I did not put in too many miles," Poulsson wrote in the report he later submitted. "I fell through the ice while crossing a river. This was the second time. Next day we tried to cross another river, but found no ice and returned, tired out, to the cabin, where Haugland told us that, at the moment he succeeded in making contact with London, his storage battery had run out. Our job depended upon our being able to find a new storage battery, for without one we could not contact London. Tronstad and Wilson would have every reason to assume we had perished or been captured."

While they were pondering what to do, Helberg returned from the summer farmhouse with a rucksack full of food: flour, meat, oats, and some dried fish. As Poulsson put it, "He proved the old Norwegian saying 'A man who is a man goes on until he can go no farther—and then goes twice as far.' "

But they had not got through to London, and the gliders were to land in less than two weeks.

Despite their exhaustion, they pushed on three more miles, to their operational base, a log cabin on Lake Sand, just east of the Skoland marshes and the Mös dam. The keeper of the dam was Einar Skinnarland's older brother, Torstein, who was also active in the underground and an old friend of Helberg's.

"After dark," Helberg said, "I'll ski over and see if Torstein can help us get a storage battery."

Meanwhile, at the Vemork heavy-water plant, another phase of the operation was being carried out.

On October 22, Jomar Brun received a telephone call at the plant from a "Mr. Berg" in Rjukan, who said he had greetings from Mikkel. Brun, a highly intelligent, delicately framed man whose quiet manner and scientific frame of mind would have disarmed the most suspicious Gestapo agent, immediately decided in favor of the unknown Mr. Berg on the strength of the word "Mikkel." Only he and Tronstad had used that code name for the latter, so Mr. Berg must have a message for him from London.

"I'll see you at my home, in an hour," Brun said.

There was still an hour's daylight left, so Mr. Berg walked the two and a half miles from Rjukan to Vemork. When he came to the suspension bridge leading to Brun's home, and the plant, on the other side of the gorge, he was allowed to cross because Brun had telephoned the German guards that he was expecting a student visitor from Oslo University. Mr. Berg was in fact Fredrik Bachke, a member of the Norwegian underground's Special Mission Command.

"I told Brun that I was there on direct orders from General Hansteen of the Norwegian High Command in London," Bachke, who is now a prominent shipowner in Trondheim, recently recalled. "He was to leave Vemork immediately and proceed to Britain to take over a very important post."

Neither Brun nor Bachke knew of the plan to sabotage the plant during the November full-moon period, but Tronstad, who had already told Brun in a letter that he might have to come to Britain, did know about it. Tronstad naturally did not want his friend to be at the plant when the British commandos attacked it, so the order to Brun to leave was carefully timed to preclude any chance of his being killed in the attack or taken hostage by the Germans after the attack was carried out.

"May I take my wife with me?" Brun asked.

"Yes," Bachke said. "The request was anticipated and permission is granted."

Mrs. Brun, who until then had been completely unaware of her husband's intelligence activities, agreed at once to accompany him. But what of their families? Would their parents and relatives suffer reprisals after they left?

"Very reluctantly Mr. Berg agreed to postpone our departure by two days to enable us to make preparations and plant a cover story," Brun has explained. "I decided to write some letters to my family and Norsk Hydro, pretending that I was suffering from a mental disorder and leaving the country to look for a new job in Sweden. We did not learn until after the war that our departure caused much trouble for our families. They were interrogated and their homes searched, but nobody was imprisoned or punished. Our own belongings were of course taken by the Nazi police."

When Bachke explained how, when, and where the Bruns were to meet their contacts in Oslo, it was as if he were drawing an uncertain graph of their future. Would they ever reach Britain or meet Mr. Berg again? Since there was no way of knowing and nothing to be gained by fretting about it, Mrs. Brun planned what Bachke later called "a jolly going-away party, just for the three of us. From the cellar she brought up canned fruit, an excellent leg of mutton, and a precious bottle of wine, all things she had been saving, and with the vegetables she had on hand prepared a dinner the like of which I had not had since before the war. We spent a merry evening together, and one thing still sticks in my mind. Mrs. Brun had just gotten a new sewing machine. She had not even tried it out, and she hated having to leave it behind."

The next morning Brun accompanied Bachke across the suspension bridge. "We were not checked by the German sentinels because they knew me," Brun later said. "On the other side we were joined by a small crowd of gay school children. This may have helped to confirm our 'innocence' in the eyes of the Germans."

After Bachke's departure for Oslo, Brun collected additional drawings, reports, and photographs that he thought would be useful in London. He also stole two kilos of heavy water and obtained poison ampules, from the Rjukan apothecary, a friend of his, to be taken in the event he and his wife were caught during their flight.

"My wife and I left Rjukan for Oslo by train on October 24, 1942," Brun recalled. "I had asked my superior, Rjukan Director Bjårne Nilssen, for leave to visit an Oslo eye specialist. In Oslo we spent the night in a hotel room, and the next morning I appeared as instructed at the Holstein suburb station, carrying the latest copy of the Nazi newspaper, *Fritt Folk,* in my coat pocket.

"A man carrying the same newspaper in his pocket approached me, and we exchanged certain catchwords which I have since forgotten. At any rate, I gave him the address of our hotel, and that evening he dropped by to tell us that we were to be transferred the next day by car to a secret flat for cover."

The next evening, after being driven through the blacked-out cobblestoned streets of Oslo in an intricately roundabout way on the chance that they were being shadowed, the Bruns arrived at a modernly furnished flat decorated with many pictures by the painter Kai Fjeld.

"The host appeared during the evening meal," Brun said, "but did not give his name. After the war we learned that he was Salve Staubo, a civil engineer."

The following day they were taken to the Oslo railway station, given tickets to Hamar, and told to get off at Stange, the station before Hamar. From Stange they were taken in a wood-burning motorcar to a farm in Romedal, where a splendid dinner had been prepared for them. From then on, led by one Norwegian guide after another, they slept in remote barns, trudged through forests, and crossed rivers.

"At the Swedish border we burned our passports," Brun recalled. "After a couple of hours on Swedish soil we met people who rang up the local sheriff. He came along in his car and took us to the local jail, where we gave our names as Sverre and Sigrid Hagen. Afterwards we were disinfected, the Swedes being afraid of typhus. . . . Later, from a concentration camp for Norwegian refugees, I called Captain Heyerdahl-Larsen at the Norwegian Embassy in Stockholm, telling him of my orders from General Hansteen to proceed to Britain as quickly as possible."

The embassy had the Bruns released immediately, obtained hotel accommodations for them in Stockholm, and after a delay of several days, due to the poor air connection between Sweden and Britain, got them aboard a plane at Broome airfield.

The Bruns took off for Britain on November 9, and it was on that same day, up on Hardanger Plateau, that Jens Poulsson and his men (with a storage battery supplied by Torstein Skinnarland) finally made radio contact with London.

"It was eerie in that solitary cabin in the wilderness to listen to a man in a city so far away," Poulsson says. "Knut Haugland lay in his sleeping bag, with only his sending hand exposed over the set. Our first message was to let Tronstad and Wilson know that we were alive and well. It was short and simple:

" 'Happy landing in spite of boulders everywhere. Snowstorm

and fog forced us to go down valleys. Four feet of snow made it impossible with heavy equipment to cross mountains.' "

In subsequent messages, as the men reconnoitered the target area and Haugland tested the portable Eureka to make sure it was still capable of sending out its electronic landing beam for aircraft, London was kept informed of developments. The messages were short, to prevent the Germans from picking up the location of the sending set, but were sent every day on schedule.

"German troops in area are Austrian. About ninety-two Germans are scheduled to come. Successful operation still possible."

"No telephone at any farm in area. All connections from Vemork to small central exchange easy to put out of action on night of operation. . . ."

"Eureka tested and O.K. Landing place lies near road by Skoland log cabin three miles from Mös dam and cannot be seen by Germans. Nice flat ground without trees or stones approximately seven hundred yards in length. . . ."

"Impossible for party to cycle. Depth of snow on landing place one foot. On road four inches and very hard. Snowshoes not yet necessary but should be brought. Whole march even under difficult snow conditions not more than five hours."

Every radio operator has an individual and recognizable way of manipulating the sending key, and Haugland was no exception. One man will cut a dash off shorter than another man, or prolong his dots more than usual. Such idiosyncrasies are called the operator's "fingerprints," and a record is made of them for security reasons. Haugland had no trouble getting through to London, but once, when he was forced, because of the intense cold, to manipulate the key with the almost frozen tips of his fingers projecting from his sleeping bag, the man receiving the message in London thought the Gestapo had captured the sending station on Hardanger Plateau. Haugland's fingers were so stiff that his prints did not match those on record. The man in London sent technical security checks, and Haugland replied correctly. Finally, the special security question, which had to be answered by a completely absurd reply, was sent.

"What did you see walking down the Strand in the early hours of January 1, 1941?"

When Haugland replied "Three pink elephants," London knew that all was well.

Poulsson did his best as cook with what little food was left. "Preparing meals in that hut was difficult," he later said, "since the room with the stove in it had no windows. It was dark, because we hardly ever had any lights, and as a rule we couldn't leave the door open, the way it was blowing and drifting. There was enough snow coming in anyway, through all the cracks. . . . We had a long antenna mast made out of planks which we nailed together, and it blew down time after time.

"We made fish soup—good soup, too—out of dog's food, some old dried fish that we found stored in the loft. Torstein Skinnarland also provided us with food. We were trying to eat our fill in order to regain strength after the hard going on insufficient rations during the advance. But it was like a drop in the ocean.

"One day Knut Haugland came across a lost sheep and lamb in a ravine. These we slaughtered and prepared for cooking. I remember, we fixed a delicious sheep's head soup, and I dropped the kettle on the floor just as I was about to put it on the table. The fellows were not in the best of humor as we crawled around on the floor, lapping up the soup and gnawing on bones."

On the night of November 17, after the moon period started, their message to London read like an invitation to the British commandos waiting in Scotland.

"Lake covered with ice and partly covered with snow. Larger lakes are ice free. Last three nights sky absolutely clear with moonlight. Temperature about 23° Fahrenheit. Strong wind from north has died down tonight. Beautiful weather."

5 Two days later, at Wick airfield in Scotland, the thirty-four specially trained commandos, all in their early twenties and all volunteers, jammed into two Horsa gliders with their equipment, guns, food, and explosives. Morale was extremely high, the atmosphere tense, and the banter good-natured and rapid-fire. That morning, a meteorological expert had promised thick cloud cover over most of the 400-mile route to the Norwegian coast, but clear skies and a full moon over the objective. With the possibility of weather conditions deteriorating for the remainder of the November moon period, the squadron's commanding officer decided to mount the operation that night.

It was drizzling but still light when the first Halifax-glider tandem left the ground, circled the airfield, and headed across the North Sea for Norway. Thirty minutes later the second glider took off behind its Halifax tug and headed in the same easterly direction. To this day no one knows with certainty exactly what happened in the grim hours that followed. The Halifax crews had been flying only Whitley and Wellington bombers up to the time they were assigned to this top-priority mission; the glider pilots, skilled as they were, therefore had little time to practice with them and attain the high standard of co-ordination required.

Running through the center of each towing line was a telephone cable that connected each Halifax with the glider behind it. Shortly after take-off, these telephone links between both Halifaxes and their gliders failed. The two Halifaxes nevertheless continued on course, the second one flying low across the North Sea to get under the cloud cover in the hope of gaining altitude as soon as the sky cleared over Norway. A landfall was made near Egersund as planned, and after clearing the first ridge of mountains, the second Halifax headed toward Rjukan. But after traveling only about ten miles farther inland, the glider crash-landed in the mountains northeast of Helleland.

Seconds later, the Halifax, after just managing to hop over the same mountain, crashed into an adjoining mountain five miles away. This suggests that the Halifax let go the tow rope in a desperate effort to gain enough altitude to clear the first mountain. Given the faulty telephone cable in the towing line, the Halifax pilot would thus have had only emergency light signals with which to warn the glider pilot that the line was about to be let go. The sudden and unexpected weight of the line on the nose of the glider must therefore have contributed to its crash-landing. In any case, the Halifax did clear the first mountain, though not the second. All four men aboard were killed instantly, and in the glider three were killed.

German troops reached the area at ten minutes before six that morning. They found fourteen surviving commandos—six of them grievously wounded in the crash—and handed them over to German battalion headquarters at Egersund. After a brief interrogation, during which each man stated his name, rank, and service number, they were ruled to be under the jurisdiction of the Führer's Commando Order, which read:

"Because of the growing number of cases in which planes are used for the landing of saboteurs, and the great damage the saboteurs have done, I hereby order that crews of sabotage planes are to be shot at once by the troops isolating them."

In accordance with this order, they were led out that evening and shot by a German firing squad. All clothes were removed from the bodies, which, together with the bodies of the men killed in the crash, were then taken a few miles farther north to the sand dunes of Brusand, a short distance north of Ogna. A trench was dug in the sand, and the bodies were thrown in. No decent burial was in any way attempted. The grave was neither marked nor tended.

The seventeen bodies at Ogna were exhumed in July 1945, and were reburied by men of their own units on July 19, with full military honors, the coffins covered with Union Jacks and roses beforehand, in the quiet cemetery of Egenes, on the outskirts of Stavanger. Many men who had served with them in earlier days made up the guard of honor. A large crowd of Norwegian civilians attended the funeral, and in the town of Stavanger all flags flew at half-mast.

The first Halifax-glider tandem had better luck, at least on its flight to the target. After take-off from Wick, in Scotland, the pilot headed southeast to get through holes in the cloud layer, then changed course several times in an effort to find the best part of the sky in which to gain altitude. The flight across the North Sea was otherwise uneventful, and as the tandem passed over Skagerrak Strait at 10,000 feet and crossed the southern coast of Norway, the sky cleared. After a few minutes, the Halifax pinpointed its position and set a northwesterly course to follow a line of lakes toward the target. Though map reading was extremely difficult, the aircraft's position was accurately known for about halfway from the coast to the target. From that point on, despite the bright moonlight, the absence of fog in the valleys, and the scarcity of clouds, the snow-covered countryside defied all efforts to identify it by the maps at hand.

On the ground, at the landing site, Poulsson and his men, who had been informed by radio that the gliders were to arrive that night, had set up lights along both sides of the landing strip. Haugland had rigged the portable Eureka, put on the earphones, and turned on the power. When the aircraft picked up the beam, Haugland would hear a special tune through the earphones and thereby know that the plane was on the way in.

"It was overcast, but the moon was full," Poulsson remembered. "We ran our Eureka battery for four hours, and our landing lights were on. Flares would have been more effective, but our lights were battery-powered."

At 2300 hours, Haugland heard the telltale tune that meant a plane was on the beam. The others could in fact hear the engines of a heavy aircraft, though they could not see it through the clouds. It came almost overhead and then circled away, as though it had just released its glider and was heading back to Britain. They waited, expecting at any moment to hear the swishing sound that heralds a landing glider, but none came.

The Halifax pilot, without knowing exactly where he was, had indeed turned the plane over the target, in the hope of getting a bearing on one of the larger, more identifiable lakes in the area. These were not seen, so course was set southeast to another line of lakes. But owing to inaccurate shapes on the map, these lakes, too, were not recognized until the southern coast came into sight about twenty miles ahead.

The crew again accurately pinpointed their position and turned back toward the target, along the now recognized line of lakes. But since they were once more flying away from the moon, with the light coming in from behind the fuselage rather than from up ahead of the pilot's cabin, map reading again became difficult, and finally, twenty miles from the target, impossible. By this time the cloud layer had begun to thicken. Since there was barely enough fuel remaining to get bomber and glider home, course was set for Scotland. The aircraft was flying at approximately 9,000 feet, some height having been lost when the second pilot took over. The clouds ahead extended to 10,000 feet, but it was extremely difficult to gain altitude without going into take-off revolutions and full boost.

Gradually the plane climbed to 12,000 feet, going through the tops of some thin cloud and then running into higher cloud, where it began to collect ice. Although the engines were set at take-off revolutions and full throttle, it became impossible to maintain height or even speed. The plane sank into the tops of clouds, where more ice formed. It was now absolutely essential to get down to below the freezing level, and to do that the pilot had to go down through ever-thickening clouds in an area abounding in mountain peaks. All lights were put full on as the aircraft went steadily down to 7,000 feet, with the glider, full of young men fighting anxiety, following close behind. The clouds became denser, the turbulence more violent, and the ice on the aircraft and towline thicker. After three violent surges, during which great strain was put on both plane and glider, the completely iced towline parted. By then they were so close to the coastline that the Halifax immediately radioed back to Britain that the glider had fallen into the sea. Actually, though, the glider was still over land. It swerved downward, through fog and zero visibility, to crash-land on top of the snow-covered mountains overlooking Lyse Fjord.

When the men aboard came to, those who were not so badly wounded looked after the others, but they could not do much. Eight men had been killed, and of the injured, one man had a spinal injury and was paralyzed from the hips down, another had two broken legs, another facial cuts and a broken jaw, and another a fractured skull, fever, and poor respiration. It was dark and bitterly cold, and they did not know where they were. Not until morning did two of the five uninjured men manage to find a farm with a telephone and make themselves understood that they needed a doctor.

When the doctor came and the two British commandos explained the situation to him, he immediately called for more medical help but warned that the Gestapo would have to be informed. He spoke English fluently and was undoubtedly giving the two young men a last chance to escape. With the civilian clothes they were wearing under their uniforms, the two commandos might have made it to Sweden. But they did not want to leave their comrades. When the Wehrmacht and the Gestapo arrived, they, too, were taken away, to Stavanger County Jail, while German soldiers and Norwegian civilians buried the eight dead Britons in a communal grave and marked it with a simple wooden cross. After the Germans left, the Norwegians fenced off the grave to prevent cattle from wandering over the ground. They planted flowers at the head, and in the summer of 1945, when a party of Royal Engineers came to investigate the tragedy, they found the grave well tended and still in excellent condition.

After the prisoners arrived at Stavanger County Jail, a dispute developed between the Wehrmacht and the Gestapo as to who had jurisdiction over them. The Army claimed that because the prisoners had been captured in British battle dress *they* had jurisdiction. The prisoners were enemy soldiers and should be treated as such— that is, sent to a prisoner-of-war camp. The Gestapo argued that the prisoners were saboteurs, that they were wearing civilian clothing beneath their uniforms and were thus technically "spies." Besides, the glider's wreckage contained snowshoes, tents, rucksacks, machine and Tommy guns, a large quantity of food, Norwegian ration cards, and Norwegian money in various denominations, which indicated an intention on the prisoners' part to remain as civilians. In addition, there were radio transmitters, explosives, and considerable quantities of sabotage material and industrial equipment. Even more revealing was the map found on one of the commandos. It was an escape map with Vemork ringed in blue ink! This eliminated any doubt the Germans may have had about the mission's target. All evidence pointed to sabotage of the Vemork plant, Germany's only source of heavy water. Therefore, the Führer's Commando Order applied.

By this time the precipitous execution of the Britons from the other Halifax-glider tandem had been brought to the attention of Reich Commissar Josef Terboven and General Wilhelm Rediess, chief of the Gestapo in Norway, who angrily made note of the fact that Hitler's Commando Order did not preclude interrogation before execution. As a result, the four seriously injured commandos were taken first to Stavanger Hospital and later to Gestapo headquarters, presumably for questioning. There, when it became apparent that they were in no condition even to be tortured, they were poisoned by a German medical officer. Their weighted bodies were taken out into the fjord, one hour's sailing time from Stavanger, and dumped overboard, never to be found again.

The five uninjured Britons were transferred to Grini concentration camp, thirty-five miles north of Oslo's shopping center. Placed first in separate cells and then all in the same cell, they were questioned many times, singly and as a group, by an English-speaking Luftwaffe officer who told them that they would soon be sent to a prisoner-of-war camp, since it had been proved that they were British soldiers. All this time, the five commandos were in close contact with another prisoner, a Norwegian corporal named Eric Dahle, and it is from him that these details are known.

After the Luftwaffe officer and the Gestapo had used "persuasion" to convince the prisoners to tell all they knew, a "Special German Delegation" came to Grini to interview the five men. For this they were handcuffed and led blindfolded from their cell (this was the last time Eric Dahle saw them) to another part of the building, where they were allowed to stand at ease, still handcuffed and blindfolded, while waiting for the interview to begin. When the Special German Delegation (actually an execution squad) arrived, the men were called to attention. The word used was *"Achtung,"* and for the execution squad it was the order to fire. The men were buried at Trandum with a British seaman and some Norwegian civilians who had suffered a similar fate.

This ended the first attempt to sabotage Germany's vital source of heavy water, and made an open secret of the fact that the Germans and the Allies were both working along the same lines in atomic research. If the Allies were willing to mount such a hazardous glider mission to destroy Germany's capacity to construct an atomic bomb, the Allies, too, must be in the process of trying to construct one. Worse still, from the Allies' point of view, there could no longer be any German doubt about the vital importance of the Vemork heavy-water plant. It was still intact after an ambitious and costly attempt to destroy it had failed, so the Germans would have ample time, before another attempt to destroy it was made, to strengthen tenfold the defenses and the garrison protecting it.

For the Allies, the question was: Should they try to bomb it from the air, with all the civilian casualties that would inevitably result, or should one last sabotage attempt be made?

6 "The November 20th wireless message about the glider disaster was a hard blow," Poulsson wrote in his report. "It was sad and bitter, especially as the weather in our part of Norway improved during the following days. . . ."

In London, Colonel Wilson, who had opposed the glider operation from the start, called Combined Operations, expressed his sympathy, and said that the latest information led him to believe that the job could be done by a small party of Norwegians, all expert skiers. Jomar Brun had arrived in Britain a week earlier and was now in a position to offer invaluable advice and assistance to just such a small-scale attack. It was, indeed, Brun's "latest information" about the plant and its layout that made Wilson think that the assignment should be given to SOE's Norwegian Section.

"Could we take over the responsibility?" he asked.

"Thank God. Please do," the officer at Combined Operations said.

That same morning, Wilson met with Tronstad, and after discussing with him the risks and possibilities, telephoned SOE's Norwegian Section in Scotland. He wanted Norwegian Lieutenant Joachim Rönneberg, he said, "to stand by for a particularly dangerous enterprise." The twenty-two-year-old Rönneberg (now a broadcasting executive in Ålesund, Norway) was to select five expert skiers from the Royal Norwegian Army's volunteers. They were to join Poulsson and his men after they parachuted onto Hardanger Plateau.

Wilson then went to Major-General Gubbins, of SOE, and told him what he had done. Gubbins reacted as he had earlier to news of the glider disaster, with shock and dismay. "You can't do that!" he said. "It's too difficult."

"I have already appointed the leader," Wilson went on, "and he is selecting the five others who will be going with him. I'm positive the job can be done, and it *will* be done." This was one of several occasions, Wilson later recalled, when he played his age against military seniority. And it worked. Within hours, the launching of a small-scale sabotage operation by SOE's Norwegian Section won the blessing of the British War Cabinet. That night, Wilson and Tronstad took the overnight express to Scotland to brief Rönneberg on the general nature of the target, the training that would be necessary, and the equipment the men would need. They even went so far as to tell him of the disastrous attempt to destroy the Vemork plant made by glider-borne troops.

"One plane crashed, and one returned to base," Wilson said. "Both gliders are missing, and according to reports we have received from Sweden, the prisoners from at least one of the gliders were shot by the Germans, although they were all in uniform."

It was highly unusual to give a soldier information about an operation with which he was not connected, but Wilson and Tronstad had agreed that in this case, if Rönneberg was to choose the right men, an exception would have to be made. For one thing, the men he chose would be operating against the same target, and, for another, it was essential that they be forewarned that if caught they could expect the same treatment from the Germans, who would now be much better prepared to protect the target from attack.

Joachim Rönneberg was a good listener and a fluent speaker, with a perfect command of English, a language required of all Norwegian school children but mastered by few. He nodded as Wilson spoke and occasionally asked a question or two, in a deep, raucous voice that somehow seemed connected with the highly developed muscles around his mouth and jaw. He also had a habit of moving his shoulders and arms when he spoke, like an athlete warming up with a ball, and when he did, his stiff, impeccable uniform seemed to creak and crackle under the hidden influence of his strength. It was almost as if both he and his body were talking.

"When SOE's Norwegian Section first started," Wilson said later, "men of the commando type were recruited. But after our sabotage work got underway in Norway, many of them had to be transferred to the regular Norwegian armed forces. However brave and efficient these men were, it began to be realized that other abilities and qualities were required. The tough gangster type of detective fiction was of little use, and, in fact, likely to be a danger. Help and support to Norwegian resistance could only be provided by men of character, who were prepared to adapt themselves and their views—even their orders at times—to other people and other considerations, once they saw that change was necessary. Common sense and adaptability are the two main virtues required in anyone who is to work underground, assuming a deep and broad sense of loyalty, which is the basic essential."

The Norwegians at SOE's training camp at Glenmore in Scotland were from all different walks of life. Except for their nationality, they had no more in common than people picked at random from one of Oslo's busy streets would have had. It was their shared determination to free their country of the Germans and their love for their king, Haakon VII, who visited them regularly and persisted in seeing them individually when they returned from a mission in Norway, that made their heterogeneousness a galvanizing agent.

Once informed of the special nature of the mission, code-named "Gunnerside," Rönneberg had no trouble choosing the five men he wanted to go with him. He approached each one individually, told him of the dangers involved in the mission, the skiing ability required, and the great importance attributed to its success.

His first choice was Lieutenant Knut Haukelid, twenty-nine years old, a powerful man with a chest built so high with sinew and muscle that it looked almost bullet-proof, a hunter's love of the outdoors, and a philosophical turn of mind—a kind of Henry David Thoreau with brawn. His unidentical twin sister was the internationally known actress Sigrid Gurie, who shared his anti-Nazi views with equal fervor.

Next came Sergeant Fredrik Kayser, a slender, wiry man as far removed from the "gangster type of detective fiction" as anyone at the camp. Active, athletic, devoted, and intelligent, he was someone Rönneberg knew he could count on when tension and danger mounted.

The Lieutenant then chose Sergeant Hans Storhaug, another unassuming, "unheroic-looking" man, neither brawny nor tall nor powerful, but with that special quality of common sense that Rönneberg was looking for. Storhaug became affectionately known as "The Chicken" by his comrades after he was caught by a Scottish gamekeeper, literally red-handed, gutting a pheasant. Though Storhaug slipped free with his prize in hand, the gamekeeper rushed down to headquarters and complained of the incident.

"Can you positively identify this man?" asked the officer in charge.

"Aye, that I can," the gamekeeper said. "He had a great ruddy beak and looked just like a chicken!"

"Rönneberg's next choice for Gunnerside was Lieutenant Kasper Idland, who later moved to Huntington, Long Island, where he died in the late '60's. Another "unheroic type" whose quiet intensity matched his brooding hatred of the Nazis, he was anxious to contribute in some way, in any way, no matter how dangerous, to the freeing of his country. Indeed, his desire for action led him to remain silent when the question of his skiing ability was raised. The great majority of Norwegians learn to ski as children, and continue to ski throughout their lives. Skis are as common in Norway as bicycles are in Holland. It was therefore taken for granted that a finely conditioned man like Idland could ski, and he said nothing to dispel that impression. Telling the truth—that he could barely ski at all—might have been interpreted as an attempt on his part to avoid taking part in such a dangerous mission. Allowing the falsehood to stand would at least give him the chance to do something against the Nazis; he put no faith in the idea of escaping to Sweden on skis anyway.

The last man picked was Sergeant Birger Strömsheim, a shy man who complemented the much more dominating Rönneberg in a way that benefited both. He spoke little, listened carefully, and seemed far removed from violence in both temperament and physical make-up. All the same, he was capable, if all the others were killed, of carrying out the sabotage operation by himself.

"We didn't know the importance of the atom at the time," Rönneberg recalls. "We just knew that our mission was extremely important—top priority—and that an air bombardment would be next if we, like the glider attempt, didn't succeed."

The six men were transferred to a special training school, Number 17, which had been cleared of all other training personnel. Because the correct identification of the target machinery was of the utmost importance, an exact wooden mock-up of the eighteen high-concentration cells was constructed, under Jomar Brun's direction, in a well-guarded hut inside the compound. Rönneberg and his men ceaselessly practiced laying dummy charges in the dark and getting the general feel of the model. They took part in drills to improve their speed and skill and to familiarize themselves with the wires, fuses, detonators, and explosives needed. They pored over aerial photographs of the hydro plant and gorge, studied diagrams of the buildings, and fashioned two complete sets of plastic explosives and detonators, each set containing one charge for each of the eighteen high-concentration cells in the basement of the huge hydroelectrolysis building.

"Sometimes we asked questions that Tronstad could not answer," Rönneberg later said. "Whenever that happened, he jotted the questions down, and the next day he had the answers for us. We never asked him about it, and he never explained. It was obvious to all of us that he had a direct line to someone who knew the heavy-water plant even better than he did."

The "someone" was, of course, Brun, who had an office right next to Tronstad's, and who indeed did have more up-to-date information about the plant than Tronstad did. The high-concentration room in the basement of the building had been expanded only a few months earlier under his direction; he knew exactly where the high-concentration cells were located, what they looked like, how much distance separated one from another, and where explosives would do the most damage. Having just recently left the plant, he also knew the exact location in the yard of the German barracks, and where the men covering the attacking party could hide. All the steel doors leading into the plant would be locked, he said, but there was one "unlocked entrance" that he strongly advised Tronstad to tell the men to use. If they used explosives to break down one of the steel doors, the noise would undoubtedly result in a gun battle with the German guards, many casualties, and, in the end, reprisals against the population. The unlocked entrance, on the other hand, had no door at all. It was a cable duct leading from outside the plant into the basement of the building. Brun knew about it because, shortly before his departure from Vemork, there had been a leak in one of the pipes carrying caustic down into the high-concentration room. In order to inspect the leak, he had had to crawl through the duct, which led from outside the building to a manhole in the ceiling of a room in the basement adjacent to the high-concentration room itself.

"There was just enough space for a person to crawl," Brun recalled, "but it represented the only unlocked entrance to the plant. Very few people even at Vemork knew about this entrance. . . ."

During all this time, none of the men chosen for the Gunnerside mission knew of Brun's presence in Britain, and Tronstad did not enlighten them, knowing that Brun's parents were living in Norway under the surveillance of German agents who still did not know that their scientist son had succeeded in reaching London. Though Tronstad trusted Rönneberg and his men completely, he did not want to burden them with secrets the Gestapo might some day force them to share. Nor did Rönneberg and his men want to be burdened with the name of Tronstad's contact, haunted as they were by the thought of leaving a traceable series of links that might jeopardize the lives of other loyal Norwegians. The more gaps there were in what they knew about others involved in the mission, the less help they would be to the Gestapo if they were captured and broke down under torture. To prevent this from happening, each man was to be supplied with a suicide capsule powerful enough to insure almost instant death the moment it was crushed between his teeth. But on such a mission, a man could be wounded, or knocked unconscious, or simply overpowered. The pill might be taken from him before he was able to use it.

Miles away, in Chicago, Illinois, the importance of the Gunnerside mission was suddenly underscored by a scientific event of unprecedented significance for all mankind. For over a month, a group of scientists had been assembling a huge collection of graphite, uranium, and uranium oxide on the floor of a squash court in a windowless cellar beneath the West Stands of Stagg Field at the University of Chicago. Every day hundreds of unsuspecting students passed the ivy-covered, neo-Gothic stadium, on Ellis Avenue between Fifty-sixth and Fifty-seventh Streets, on Chicago's South Side. They had no way of knowing what was going on inside, for although all doors leading to the squash court were kept locked, no guards were stationed outside to attract attention or cause gossip. Security was in fact so tight that not even the president and the trustees of the university were aware that an experiment capable of producing highly intense radioactive materials, equivalent to tons of radium, was being carried out on their campus.

General Leslie Groves himself, the man carrying the ultimate responsibility for this project, had "serious misgivings about the wisdom" of carrying out the experiment in the heart of Chicago. "If the pile should explode," he said, "no one knew just how far the danger would extend. Stagg Field lies in the heart of a populous area. . . ."

Among the scientists assigned to the experiment, there was a sense of urgency and fear, of dedication and purpose. As atomic physicist Samuel Goudsmit put it: "Since the Germans had started their uranium research about two years before us, we figured they must be at least two years ahead of us. They might not have the bomb yet, but they must have had chain-reacting piles going for several years. It followed that they must have fearful quantities of artificial radioactive materials available. How simple it would be for them to poison the water and food supplies of our large cities with chemically non-detectable substances and sow death wholesale among us by dreadful invisible radiations.

"The fear was so real that the scientists were even sure of the place and the date of Hitler's supposed radioactive attack. The Germans must know, they thought, that Chicago was at that time the heart of our atom bomb research. Hitler, lover of dramatic action, would choose Christmas day to drop radioactive materials on that city. Some of the men on the project were so worried they sent their families to the country. The military authorities were informed and the fear spread. I heard rumors that scientific instruments were set up around Chicago to detect the radioactivity if and when the Germans attacked."

In the windowless cellar beneath the stands of Stagg Field, the work went on under the direction and supervision of physicist Enrico Fermi, a refugee from Fascist Italy, who had been awarded the 1938 Nobel Prize for physics for his experiments with radioactivity. Outstanding as an experimenter, theorist, and teacher, he worked hand in hand with the other scientists to build the gigantic latticework that was to be, they hoped, the first self-sustained chain-reacting uranium pile ever made. Built in the shape of a somewhat flattened sphere, like a huge doorknob, it was supported by a timber framework resting on the floor of the squash court, whose backcourt and service line were still visible. For weeks they worked from early morning until late at night, building the graphite bricks up in layers, while Fermi placed the lumps of uranium and uranium oxide at carefully calculated distances through the graphite to form the lattice.

On December 1, with the eleventh layer finished, the structure was close to being three-quarters complete. Already weighing many tons, it might, with the next layer, or the layer after that, go critical. When that happened, the freed neutrons, slowed down but not captured by the graphite, would collide with and split up uranium 235 atoms, which in turn would give rise to more neutrons, which again would explode more and more atoms, until the reaction would sustain itself. But the neutron counters still showed no sign of a neutron multiplication factor greater than one.

Fermi, who had been given the name "Dr. Farmer" for security reasons, retired that evening shortly after eleven, leaving Dr. W. H. Zinn in charge. No one expected any reaction in the pile until it was nearer completion, but as Zinn and others worked into the night, piling pieces of uranium and bricks of graphite to make the twelfth layer of the structure, someone heard what seemed to be a change in the tempo of the clicks coming from the neutron counters. With each additional piece of uranium and brick of graphite added to the pile, the tempo of the clicks seemed to increase. If the counters were to be believed, the neutrons were definitely coming out at a faster rate.

"We knew then," Zinn later recalled, "that if we pulled out the control rods, the thing would pop. But we did not want to wake Dr. Fermi."

The control rods passed through slots in the pile at ten different places. Boron-carbide rods ran through the three slots near the center of the pile; neutron-absorbing cadmium strips, used for experimentation and added safety, ran through the other seven slots. It was believed that any one of the cadmium strips was capable of absorbing enough of the freed neutrons to keep the chain reaction within bounds, but because the experiment was being carried out in the heart of one of America's largest cities, the scientists used every precaution to prevent an explosion and possible radioactive contamination.

Early the next morning, Fermi was there as usual, with Arthur H. Compton, Eugene Wigner, Leo Szilard, and the other scientists working on the project. The news of what had happened during the night had alerted everyone to the possibility that one of the great moments in history might be near, and when the control rods and neutron-absorbing cadmium strips were carefully removed from the slots in the pile and checked, the measurements did show that neutrons were being released at a faster rate than had been anticipated for the twelfth layer of the pile. Fermi and his associates slipped the rods and strips back in the slots and began adding more bricks of graphite and lumps of uranium and uranium oxide to the top layer of the pile. Readings were taken at frequent intervals on the neutron counters—readings that seemed to keep pace with their progress. The tension and excitement kept increasing, until it was as if they were using the actual physical task at hand—the bending, lifting, and climbing—as a buffer between themselves and their emotions. The Germans might already have produced their own nuclear chain reaction, but no one knew that for sure, so this one, if they succeeded, might well be the first in history.

By noon they were agreed that the goal might be near. The pile by then had grown to consist of 350 tons of the purest graphite, five and a half tons of uranium, and thirty-six and a half tons of uranium oxide, all of it intricately latticed in what they hoped would be the proper balance. Another hour or two and the pile should be on the brink of going critical.

After lunch they worked at a slower pace and with even greater care, to reduce the chance of failure or disaster. Fermi himself placed the last pure uranium eggs in the corners of the graphite matrix. Then all of the control rods and all but one of the cadmium strips were pulled out. Finally, the one remaining cadmium strip was slowly pulled out, and in the next fraction of a second, some of the uranium-235 nuclei in the pile were split by flying neutrons. This produced more neutrons, some of which bombarded and split other uranium-235 nuclei, which in turn released more and more neutrons. The intensity of the neutrons emitted by the pile began to increase rapidly. Click, click, click went the neutron counters, as the reaction reached critical dimensions and began to go on all by itself. Faster and faster came the neutrons, clocked by the ever-increasing clicks of the counters.

Dr. Fermi, who, with his Jewish wife, had never returned to Italy after receiving his Nobel Prize in Stockholm, stood intently by the instrument recording the number of neutrons per minute. Faster and faster came the clicks, keeping pace with the flying, multiplying neutrons. For a moment he stood as if alone, as the fission-producing neutrons began multiplying themselves by the constant factor of 1.006. This meant that for each neutron that went into the splitting of one U-235 atom, more than one neutron was produced to carry on the process of splitting more U-235 atoms. A self-sustained chain-reacting uranium pile, and with it the awesome energy of atomic power—100 million times more than the energy produced by the ordinary burning of an atom— had become a reality.

General Groves was en route east from the Pacific Coast at the time and could not be reached. Dr. Compton, after warmly congratulating Fermi, called Dr. James B. Conant, chairman of the National Defense Research Committee, at Harvard University. Using exactly fourteen words, he gave Conant the now famous coded message:

"The Italian navigator has just landed in the new world. The natives are friendly."

7

Although the success of the Fermi pile was one of the best-kept secrets of the war, the Germans continued to show every sign that they knew they were in a race with the Allies for an atomic bomb. For example, a week before Fermi's success in Chicago, General Rediess, from his headquarters in Norway, warned Berlin that there were "several indications that the British placed great importance on the destruction of Vemork's heavy water installations." Then, on December 4, just two days after the Chicago pile went critical, a false air-raid alarm was sounded in Rjukan, and while the townspeople sought shelter, 200 German troops entered the town and searched every house.

"The search lasted for fifteen hours, on December 4th, during which a state of siege prevailed," the London *Times* reported from its news services in Stockholm.

Later that same day, Reich Commissar Terboven and General Nikolaus von Falkenhorst, the German commander in chief in Norway, drove up to Vemork and personally inspected the factory. Thus there seemed no longer to be any reason to doubt that the Germans had learned the exact objective of the glider troops. Many Norwegians were arrested, including Torstein Skinnarland, who spent the rest of the war in a concentration camp. The Rjukan garrison was strengthened, and work was begun on a mine field to be built around the plant. German police even went so far as to cordon off and search the area where the two gliders had been scheduled to land.

Luckily, Poulsson and his men anticipated trouble long before the police arrived. "We didn't feel very safe where we were," Helberg has explained. "The German camp on the Mös dam was only two and a half miles away. We didn't especially appreciate the neighborhood."

Even before they learned of Torstein Skinnarland's arrest, they had left the cabin by the Skoland marshes and hurried northwest on Hardanger Plateau, spending several days at a cabin in Grasdalen, then moving farther north to a small hunting cabin— the "Cousin's Cabin," they called it, because Poulsson and his cousin had built it before the war. Situated in a kind of finger-lakes region at Saure, about eighteen miles northwest of the Rjukan valley, it was neither marked on the map nor near anything resembling a trail.

"In a table drawer I found the guest book," Poulsson recalls. "I leafed through it, smiling somewhat painfully. I knew the names, and found my own. My last time in the cabin was the summer of 1939. . . ."

Earlier they had been told by London to await further orders, that another attacking party would be arriving. Only one plane would be used this time, they learned from subsequent messages, and not more than six men, all of them Norwegian volunteers. The men would parachute out near the Cousin's Cabin and join Poulsson's group for an attack on the plant.

"This meant there would be ten of us altogether," Helberg said. "The German guards at Rjukan and Vemork numbered somewhere between two and three hundred. Somehow, though, we figured we'd manage."

But in their radio communications with London, nothing was said about how they were to survive until the next attacking party arrived. With their only food supplier, Torstein Skinnarland, arrested, they were again close to starvation. For two weeks they lived on nothing but oatmeal, a little margarine, and reindeer moss, a whitish-brown lichen that forms carpets of growth about an inch thick over the surface of rocks and sandy soil. When Poulsson reminded his men that reindeer survived solely on this moss during the winter, they dug through the snow to get at it, then boiled it in snow water with oatmeal. Poulsson was a great believer in the nutritiousness of reindeer moss—"It's full of vitamins and minerals," he kept saying—but Helberg was skeptical.

"On this meager food, our strength and resistance to disease decreased rapidly," Helberg said. "Arne Kjelstrup and I got fat with edema. My weight increased by over twenty pounds. I had to get up six times a night to urinate."

There were times when everybody was sick in bed except Jens Poulsson, the great believer in reindeer moss, who consumed more of it than anyone else.

"I think he managed simply because he went around raving about reindeer roasts," Helberg says. " 'Just wait until there's game in the area,' he kept saying, 'then we'll have plenty to eat.' He had shot many a reindeer on the plateau before the war. The rest of us, who had scarcely seen a reindeer before, had our doubts."

From about the tenth of December, after Knut Haugland found a Krag rifle and some cartridges in a cabin on the far side of one of the many lakes in the region, Poulsson went on daily reindeer hunts. But fog kept pouring in from the east, and the higher into the mountains he skied, the thicker the fog became. Every day he returned, his rifle cold and his rucksack empty, to the sickly, unexpectant faces of his comrades, to dwindling rations and a few warm hours by the stove.

The men developed fever and suffered dizzy spells during which they lost all sense of time. They had to continue gathering firewood—that was essential—but a growing fondness for rest kept eddying them away from resolution. It became work, hard work, just to get up during the night to urinate. The cabin became a compost of body and cooking odors mixed with a variety of sickness smells. At night, either someone was coughing or the wind blew snow through crevices with such a curious quiet that it was as if the desolate plateau were sharing its secret with them.

Then came the day before Christmas, and Poulsson, as if

finding in routine itself an incentive to go on, was up again before dawn, preparing for the next hunt. Since Kjelstrup was going for firewood, he left the hut with Poulsson and lingered outside, where the snow was trampled by boots and marked by ski tracks leading from the shed, while Poulsson fastened his skis. The temperature had dropped thirty degrees during the night, and the ammonia-sharp air cut into their lungs.

"Cold and clear," Kjelstrup said. Though his red beard flamed in the sun, he did not look well. Every day he had grown weaker, more bloated with edema, and more sluggish. His glazed, borrowed-looking eyes, the whites yellow, the edges red where the tangled lashes grew, appeared more caught up in their own exertions than in focusing on anything.

Poulsson slipped his rucksack and rifle over his back and got his ski poles ready. After weeks of fruitless hunting, he had begun to doubt the very existence of reindeer on Hardanger Plateau.

"The reindeer is as native to Norway as the lion is to Africa," he said. "Only where are they?"

Raising his binoculars to his eyes, he scanned the surrounding terrain with his jaw set, as if prepared to see nothing, as usual. And, as usual, he saw nothing.

"If only I could focus on where the reindeer will be tomorrow," he said, putting the glasses away, "I could build myself a snow house and lie in wait for them."

Kjelstrup smiled, or tried to. "Maybe today will be your day."

Poulsson had skied hardly at all for four days, and his poles seemed livelier as he pushed off and glided over the rolling countryside in easy diagonal strides. The snow had a crust that broke with a crunching sound against the impact of his poles, but the skis sailed over the surface with such exhilarating speed that he felt hopeful for the first time in a week. Snow and ice like this he looked upon as friends, for they made travel both a pleasure and a continuous and rhythmic exercise. He could feel the working of the muscles in his legs, arms, abdomen, and back, and in his neck and face as well.

After poling along over the white barren terrain for about five miles, he came to a halt, his heart pounding, his breath steaming round his beard. There were reindeer tracks in the snow! They were fresh tracks, made that morning by reindeer traveling into the wind at a leisurely pace. How many were in the herd he could not estimate accurately, for reindeer have a way of stepping in one another's footsteps when the snow is deep or crusty. But from the length of their strides and from obvious signs along the trail that they had stopped to graze or rest, he estimated their traveling speed to be no more than two or three miles an hour. If he could spot them through his field glasses, he should be able to overtake them by midday. He might even be able to intercept them, for reindeer seldom alter course unless there is a change of wind.

Herringboning his way to the top of a hill to get a better view, he found a boulder to sit on, got a piece of flannel from beneath his watch band, and carefully wiped every exposed lens of his binoculars before raising them to his eyes. The landscape was well within the power of the lens, so he rested his elbows on his knees and slowly swung the glasses, one degree at a time, from left to right, then from foreground to horizon and back to foreground again to overlap one view with the next. He spent several minutes doing this, but the reindeer were nowhere in sight. Of course, they might be in some nearby valley, hidden by the crest of a hill, or up on some higher level out of his range of vision.

He decided to follow the trail and pushed off, poling along except where he could glide down gentle hills or dip and curve around obstacles. He kept crisscrossing the reindeer trail for about five more miles, always keeping a sharp lookout on the chance that he might see the herd just beyond the nearest hill. The farther he traveled, the more expectant he became, but the reindeer remained hidden. Could they have seen a wolf or picked up the scent of one and made off? If so, they could be twenty or thirty miles away by now.

Suddenly sighting some black specks at the northern end of the valley, he came to a gliding halt so as not to throw up snow or make anything resembling a crunching sound in the packed surface of it. Except for a few tattered clouds, the sky was clear, but the sun was higher now, and here and there, where it shone on various configurations of naked rock in the snowy terrain, rising air currents of different temperature and humidity created in the atmosphere a quivering, wavy motion that blurred his vision and made fantastic shapes out of what was real and what falsely appeared to be real.

Objects on the snow surface appeared out of all natural proportion; they disappeared, reappeared, and sometimes even seemed to change their relative positions. A mere turn of the head created the illusion that contours in the land had shifted, so that there was no firm idea of distance, and hence no reliable scale for comparison. In such hazy subarctic light, a small stone may look like a tall man standing off in the distance, a frightened beaver may show all the signs of being a huge bear, a broken and discarded sledge may resemble a cabin half covered with snow.

The black specks in the valley were too far off to be identified by the naked eye. They were moving, though, all in the same direction, so they could not be stones.

Reindeer, Poulsson thought. If only they're reindeer! What a Christmas present for the men.

He could almost see Kjelstrup's smile and hear Helberg's shouts at the sight of him returning to the hut with a rucksack full of venison. But before raising his field glasses to his eyes, he again wiped every exposed lens to remove any smudge that might distort his vision. There was no hurry anyway, and he knew it, for reindeer in a flock do not travel fast unless they are frightened. Like cattle, they graze, lie down for long periods, then move leisurely on to where they can graze again.

When he raised the glasses to his eyes, despite his efforts to be methodical and calm, he could feel his throat grow tight with excitement at the sight of the upward-reaching reindeer horns against the sky, the sprightly step in the virgin snow, and the round, open eyes that might in their innocence have been witnessing the dawn of time. There were old and young bulls, cows, yearlings, and two-year-olds of both sexes. Traveling at a brisk walk, the calves with restless energy, the young bucks with playful springs, and the older bucks and cows with their necks stretched far forward, the better to sniff the air in front of them, they were heading into the wind, as reindeer usually do, in order to pick up the scent of any enemy who might be lying in wait for them. Having already acquired their white winter coats, they blended in with the snowy terrain in a way that only their antlers and prancing movements betrayed.

"They were moving slowly toward Angelbutjonn Lake," Poulsson recalled. "I was to leeward of them, where they could not pick up my scent, so I took off, heading for the lake to get them within range. The hunting fever had seized me."

Because of the hilly terrain, he soon lost sight of the animals. But every now and then he caught a glimpse of their antlers like moving trees behind a rise of ground, and that was all he needed. By keeping their location and direction in mind, and using the irregular hills and ridges both as cover and as a means of increasing his skiing speed, he was able to approach them from a new direction and still remain to leeward of them.

The lake lay in a small valley running roughly north-south. When he reached the range of hills that formed the valley's western slope, he unfastened his skis and quietly crawled to the summit. Reindeer have acute powers of scent and hearing, but they cannot see very far. Even on the clearest days, they cannot see a man farther off than half a mile, and under most conditions they cannot see a man farther off than half that distance. Though Poulsson was beyond their range of vision, he crawled to a huge boulder, behind which he could stand to his full height without being seen, before getting out his glasses for a closer look.

The reindeer had settled down by the lake below. Some were grazing, others were lying on the ice, dozing and chewing their cuds, and a few were just standing there, motionless. There were over seventy of them, in an area about an acre in size, and hanging over them in the cold air was a mist from the moisture and warmth of their breathing. Poulsson was about to lower his glasses when he noticed that a smaller flock had gone up to Angelbuhord, about half a mile farther north.

"My position was hopeless," he said. "To the east and south was the open valley. I could not make my approach along either route without being seen. And to the northeast, where the terrain was favorable, with various small hills and hollows and creek beds branching off in different directions, I could not get within range without being betrayed by the wind."

There was nothing to do but wait until the herd moved on to rougher terrain, where hills, ridges, and rocks would enable him to make his approach unseen. The only trouble was the shortness of daylight at that time of year. He had left the hut that morning at nine o'clock, just as the sun appeared above the horizon. That was three hours ago, and in another three hours the sun would be gone, and with it the chance of shooting with any accuracy.

As the time passed and he tried to decide what to do, he became conscious of the steam his breath was making in the air, and of the air itself as an almost tangible thing against his skin. Guarding against frostbite, he began to "make faces," wild, exaggerated faces that wrinkled the skin around his forehead, eyes, nose, and mouth. He knew that an inactive face not only freezes faster than an active one, but often freezes without warning as well, and then bleeds if it is rubbed too hard. By continually grimacing as he watched the reindeer below, he was able to detect any stiffening spot. Whenever he did, he slipped his warm hand out of his glove, pressed the spot until the stiffness was gone, made another face to make sure the skin had thawed, and slipped his hand back inside the glove. As an added precaution, he kept wiggling his toes to check for numbness, and brushing his beard vigorously with his glove to prevent his breath from freezing in it. If his beard became imbedded with ice, he would have to return to the hut without delay to thaw it out.

He did not want to return empty-handed this time, and the limited remaining daylight only added to his impatience. When would the reindeer move to another browsing place? And when they did move, how long would it take him to stalk them? It was astounding how much moss they could devour in a day; why didn't they move on in search of more?

Having read about the unlimited patience of the eskimo in approaching reindeer for a kill, he wondered what an eskimo would do in this situation, with the low sun of the short winter day descending and the time for patience running out. He had been on too many fruitless hunts, without even seeing reindeer tracks, to remain here now and do nothing until darkness removed all chance of using his rifle. His men were getting weaker, more haggard, and less able to resist the cold with every passing day. And so was he, as his stiffening legs and empty stomach kept telling him.

He glanced at his watch. Almost half an hour had passed since the reindeer had settled by the lake, and they showed no sign of moving. In fact, now others were lying on the ice, and, to make matters worse, two young bulls were leaving their beds on the ice and straying off to a patch of reindeer moss about fifty yards closer to where he was hiding. Though they remained well out of range, they were in a better position to see him and alert the entire herd if he made a move. This was what made approaching a large herd so difficult; there were always two or three stragglers on the flanks to act as unwitting sentries.

On the slim chance that the two young bulls might move closer, he got his rifle ready. Given their age and sex, they would have lost most of their fat by this time of year, but the two of them together would more than equal an old cow or an old bull. If they remained one behind the other, as they were now, and meandered toward him that way up the hill, he might get both of them with one shot. He did not like the pointed, full-jacketed bullets he had, because they did not mushroom on impact and often, as a result, merely wounded an animal. On the other hand, one such bullet would still have killing force after going through the body of the first bull, unless it spent itself against the vertebrae or some large bone. But he had reached the point where he was willing to settle for just one bull.

If only I could get to that knoll down there, he thought, examining through his glasses a small, snow-covered rise in the ground about two hundred yards down the hill. The wind isn't much, but it's still in my favor, so they won't be able to smell me. If they'd just turn around and start back, I could get to the knoll and have plenty of time to aim. The whole herd would be in range.

Eating snow to relieve his parched mouth and throat, he waited ten, twenty minutes. Then, as the two young bulls turned toward the herd, he made his move. Leaving his rucksack, skis, and poles behind, he bent forward, with his rifle in his right hand, and took short, rapid, sometimes sliding steps downhill through the snow where there did not appear to be any rocks or stones to trip over or kick. At the same time, to his dismay, he noticed that the two young bulls had merely turned; they had not started back toward the herd. He kept getting closer to them the farther down the hill he went.

Glancing quickly and repeatedly from the slope in front of him to the two young bulls, who were standing motionless, as if enthralled by their own elongated shadows in the snow, he made it about halfway down before, as if to browse some more, they turned toward him again. He was still to leeward of them, so they could not identify him by scent as a man, and still too far away for them to identify him by sight. Both animals stared, studying him intently, as though the world and everything in it were theirs to see, sniff, examine, and enjoy. What could it be, their popping eyes seemed to say, that long treelike thing up there on the slope?

Realizing that reindeer often fail to recognize danger in anything that is not moving, Poulsson tried to stop and remain where he was, absolutely still, in the hope that they would see him, in his white ski outfit, as part of the snowy scenery. But he happened to be trying to negotiate a particularly slippery stretch. There was no chance of his stopping in his tracks. Indeed, by trying to, he almost fell, with his rifle high in the air. It was impossible for the two young bulls not to see the sudden disturbance on the hill above them, even though they could not identify the cause of it. With their poor eyes they saw him as a moving object, which meant he might be anything—a wolf, a wolverine, or even another reindeer. And that was the trouble, for they reacted as reindeer always do— on the side of caution. The oldest of the two stamped with anger, leaped into the air, came down hind legs first, and leaped again. In the next instant, he and his companion turned tail and ran as fast as they could, pounding with their hoofs and kicking up so much snow that all the others in the herd, alarmed by the commotion, wrenched themselves to their feet and pounded after them.

The calves and yearlings, faster by far than the others in the herd, led the retreat, overtaking even the two young bulls who had sounded the alarm. Then came the young cows and young bulls, and behind them the old cows. Bringing up the rear, with thunder in their hoofs, were the old bulls, handicapped by age and the weight of their huge antlers.

Seconds later, when they had disappeared behind a hill and the flying snow settled and the cloud of steam hovering over their trail vanished, it was hard to believe they had been there at all.

"I suddenly felt tired and weak," Poulsson remembered. "I swore out loud. I nearly cried."

What was he to do? Go after them? He knew that reindeer, when they see a moving object and fail to get its scent, ordinarily do not run far. Often they halt abruptly a quarter of a mile away, recover their poise, and resume grazing as though nothing had happened. Experts at scenting danger, they seem to have no memory of it.

He could follow their tracks in the hope of overtaking them before sundown, but the smaller flock, farther north, as he saw through his glasses, was still in Angelbuhord, in the same area. They were up fairly high, grazing peacefully, on a plateau stretching northward from the crest of a steep hillside.

I'll try them, he thought, while there's still time. After scrambling back up to the boulder where he had left his equipment, he quickly fastened his skis, strapped his rucksack and rifle to his back, and pushed off, traveling fast, to make the most of the precious few hours of daylight left. As he approached the hillside above which the plateau started, he took one last look at the reindeer before the crest of the hill hid them from view. They looked peaceful and content, so on reaching the foot of the hill, he unfastened his skis and rested a moment. Then he swung them and his poles over his shoulder and started trudging upward.

The slope was long and steep, and the higher he went the more his steaming breath clung in frosty molecules to his beard. Whenever he stopped to rest and brush the frost off, he could see his footsteps like a scrawled line behind him, and beyond his footsteps, his ski tracks, extending from the foot of the hill through the white desolation toward all the other hills he would have to climb on his way home. The vast land stretched into the distance, past bogs, lakes, and snow peaks beheaded by the wind toward what appeared to be a white sea continually changing shape before his eyes. He found it hard to think of the homeward trip, he felt so weak and dreamy. It was easier to think only of reaching the top of this hill and shooting a reindeer.

Take shorter steps from now on, he told himself as he continued his climb. Easier on the heart.

Near the top, he stuck his skis and poles upright in the snow and crawled the last few yards with his rifle ready.

There they are, he thought, raising his eyes just above the crest of the hill. But the wind had subsided considerably, and what was left of it was erratic; it blew this way and that, as though in the process of changing direction or dying altogether. If it changed in the wrong direction, the reindeer would pick up his scent; if it died altogether, they would be able to hear him at a farther distance than he could shoot. He had to hurry to get closer. They were still out of range and getting restless. One by one they rose to their feet and stood there, while the snow packed against their sides slipped off, leaving only a powdery covering on their backs.

By sliding headfirst down to a windrow of snow, then guardedly circling behind it to leeward, or to what he hoped was leeward in the crazy wind, he was able to get to within two hundred yards of them without being detected. His intention was to shoot the nearest animal through the body just behind the diaphragm, because an animal shot this way will usually stand still where it is hit, then lie down as if naturally and not alarm the others in the flock. The report of the rifle would be similar to the noise made by the frost cracks that form in the ground on suddenly cold days. Since leaving the cabin, he had heard several such loud, cracking sounds, caused by the mud beneath the snow splitting apart in response to the drop in temperature. Reindeer are familiar with such cracking sounds in winter, so the shot would not frighten them unless he missed and they heard the whistle of the bullet in the air or the thud of it striking the ground. If he aimed correctly and hit the nearest animal, he would be able to get at least two or three additional animals before the flock panicked and ran off.

"I got up on my knees, took careful aim, and fired," Poulsson said. "But the animal didn't fall."

Suddenly the entire flock, alerted to danger, started running straight across in front of him, toward another hill, leading upward from the level they were on.

"I shot again, twice, at two different animals," Poulsson said. "Again without result."

He could not understand it. Could the glaring sunlight on the snow have been that hard on his eyes? He aimed again, but it was too late; the entire flock, thirty animals altogether, was heading straight up the hill above him in a rain of flying snow. Then they were gone, leaving only their tracks and the steam from their bodies behind.

Angered, depressed, and puzzled by his poor shooting, Poulsson trudged aimlessly over to where the animals had been grazing. There he saw blood in the snow, in three different tracks. It was those blasted bullets! He had hit all three of the animals he had aimed at, but the nonmushrooming bullets had passed through their bodies with enough force to whistle through the air beyond them. No wonder the flock had made off.

With his steaming breath crowding round his face, he followed the bloody tracks, struggling up the hillside to still-higher altitudes in the hope of overtaking the three wounded animals before the wolverines and buzzards got to them. Less than a hundred yards beyond the top of the hill, where the terrain rolled slowly downward again, he saw one of the three wounded reindeer lying in the snow. Casting about with its head and kicking up snow in a last uneven battle with death, it was trying to get up and follow the others. Poulsson aimed one more shot and fired, this time with immediate effect. The animal, a cow, judging from the relatively slender antlers, lay absolutely still in the snow as Poulsson, exhausted now and a little dizzy, approached.

"The reindeer was a good-sized female," he said. "And when I reached her, I giggled to myself. I laughed out loud. 'So we'll be having meat, after all,' I said to myself. 'Fat meat, too.' "

Quickly getting a bucket from his rucksack, he collected as much of the blood as possible, drank a cupful or two while it was still warm, and went in search of the other reindeer he had wounded.

"I followed the tracks of the flock for a while, but the

wounded animals were nowhere in sight. Judging from the few drops of blood in the snow, and the distance between one drop and another, they were apparently able to keep up with the others. So I turned back. I hated wounding them like that, but this was no sport. It was a matter of our very existence, of carrying out the mission."

Returning to where he had killed the deer, he opened his rucksack, placed it beside him in the snow, and went to work skinning and dismembering the animal. The head and tongue he put in the rucksack first, because they were the most delicious. Then came the fatty cuts, such as the ribs and brisket, and such organs as the heart, liver, and kidneys.

"As a boy I was very interested in primitive survival," Poulsson recalled. "I read a great deal about Eskimos and American Indians and how they hunted and cooked. I learned that the parts of the animal that in civilized life are considered the choice parts are not necessarily the parts that help sustain you in survival conditions."

The leg bones he took for the marrow they contained; the visceral fat for energy and added enrichment of the meat. To keep up his strength for the homeward trip, he chewed pieces of fat while working, and now and then he would split a small bone near the toes for the marrow. In these small bones, which help give reindeer their extraordinary spring and elevation, the marrow is liquid and almost as clear as water. Poulsson drank it ravenously, with what little of the blood was not already frozen.

"The reindeer's stomach and its contents are loaded with the kind of vitamins and minerals we needed for survival," Poulsson said. "We were all suffering from serious vitamin deficiency, so I removed the stomach and its contents, altogether about fifty pounds of meat, organs, and bones."

By this time the sun was disappearing behind the mountains to the west, so he quickly spread the reindeer pelt over the lean cuts of meat, to be picked up the next day, strapped the loaded rucksack and frozen bucket of blood to his back, fastened his skis, and started back in his old tracks.

"The setting sun was gilding the highest peaks in the mountains, and the evening cold was setting in," Poulsson remembers. "I felt tired under the weight of the rucksack, but happy, too, as I poled along the same way I had come. Then, as I sped down the slope toward Angelbutjonn Lake, I came across the large herd of reindeer I had encountered that morning. They were lying on the ice in almost the exact same place, and they didn't notice me until I was right by shore. Suddenly, the entire herd, in a compact mass, started off. There was a thunder of hoofs, and a shrill, creaking sound from the rubbing together of their horns. In seconds they were gone, leaving only the trampled snow behind them. But I knew they'd be back, along with other herds migrating from the west."

It was dark when he reached the hut, and inside, in the light of the kerosene lamp, the men looked as he imagined they would: grimy, tired, weak, and unexpectant. They did not even bother to ask him about his day, so convinced were they that it had been like every other day. But then Kjelstrup, seeing blood on his white ski outfit, rushed out to the rucksack in the snow just outside the door. When he lifted it, he let out a shout that brought life to the haggard faces of Haugland and Helberg. Christmas would be a day of rejoicing, after all.

During the weeks that followed, as more reindeer migrated onto the Hardanger Plateau and hunting them became more successful, the eating habits of the men gradually changed. Living, as they were, under survival conditions, on a diet limited to venison, they began to prefer the parts of the animal they had in peacetime ignored, and to disdain the parts they had previously prized the most. Tender reindeer steaks, for example, a top peacetime item in the finest Oslo restaurants, they found dry and unsatisfying unless combined with suet and marrow. Reindeer fat, a thing they had avoided before, became a routine part of every meal, for the good reason that it was essential to the digestive process itself, given the sub-zero temperatures and the high protein content of the meat. Besides, with such fat equivalents as sugar and starch absent from their diet, they discovered subtle differences in fat, as well as in bone marrow, and soon became experts in the fine variations in the flavor of both.

The most delicious fat they found to be just behind the eyes; the clearest and most delectable marrow they discovered in the small bones nearest the hoof. In this same slender part of the hind leg, just below the kneecap, they also found a small but special lump of fat, and, between the bones themselves, the most luscious meat.

In time, like experienced hunters of the north who live exclusively on game, they began to judge meat by its flavor rather than by its tenderness. Except for the barren female reindeer, whose meat is a gourmet's delight, they found the bulls the best eating, especially the old bulls, with their rich, fatty, tasty meat. The cows came next, then the calves, with their tender but bland, less flavorful meat.

As to the different cuts of meat, the men disagreed in a way that added zest to the passing of time while they awaited the arrival of Gunnerside. They all agreed that the head of the animal was best, for it contained the brains, the fat behind the eyes, the nerves of the teeth, the tongue, the nose and lips, with their oddly delicious chestnut flavor, and the eyes themselves, which they fried in fat until brown and crisp. The brisket, ribs, and vertebrae came next, in that order. Some preferred the heart to the kidneys, others preferred the meat near the bone in the neck or the shoulders if it was not cooked too long.

Kidney fat was chosen over brisket fat, which in turn was

preferred over intestinal fat. Last, and least agreeable, they all agreed, was back fat, which also made the hardest tallow. The tastier the fat, indeed, the softer the tallow it made.

Of course, these distinctions did not deter them from using the entire animals, from hoofs to horns, even including the pelts, which they spread over the floor boards to help keep out the cold. Leftover bones were pounded, then boiled with the hoofs in a kettle for forty-eight hours. When the resulting liquid was strained and allowed to cool, it turned into a thick, protein-rich gelatin that they always added, every morning at breakfast, to the porridge they made of the blood, the tissues of the larynx, and the vitamin-rich contents of the stomach.

"When it's a matter of survival," Poulsson said, "your taste and appetite change to fit your body's needs. One day someone killed a yearling. Well, no one liked the contents of the yearling's stomach, because when reindeer graze in winter, the yearling is relegated to the thin, outer edges of the reindeer moss, where the earth is sandy. But when we started to eat the animal, we ate the stomach contents, too. It was like eating sand, but what else could we do? We needed the vitamin C."

From this point on, while waiting for the Gunnerside party to parachute onto the plateau and join them for the attack, they hunted, gathered firewood, kept in contact with London, and lived exclusively on reindeer meat and oatmeal. Every day was like every other day, or as Poulsson described a morning at the Cousin's Cabin in his notebook:

"Shivering with cold, I crawl out of my sleeping bag, stick my feet in my moccasins, light the kerosene lamp, and drop down on the stool by the stove. It is seven-thirty, and today it is my turn to fix breakfast.

"Cut-up shavings and dry wooden sticks are ready for use, and soon there are crackling sounds and rays of heat coming from the stove. When the stones inside begin to warm, I start burning damp wood and put the meat kettle and the oatmeal porridge on to heat. The meat as well as the porridge are ready-made from last night. They only need a quick boil.

"Meanwhile, I get my clothes on, take the hatchet and kettle, and go outside. It is still dark, but clear and sparklingly cold. In the snowbank by the cabin wall, the reindeer stomach is buried. It is frozen and hard as a rock, but I chop off a few good-sized chunks, put them in the kettle, and hurry inside.

" 'The porridge is ready,' I call out. From dark corners come a couple of grunts in reply, but soon the men are sitting on the edge of the beds pulling their clothes on. They make a quick dash outdoors before gathering around the breakfast table.

"The porridge is served and the meat ready on the table. Only the 'guts' are still on the stove. Few words are exchanged. We eat. A big plate of porridge and then two big plates of reindeer loin with lots of suet. And with the meat we eat the 'guts'—wonderful, green, reindeer-stomach contents with plenty of vitamin C. There is prosperity now.

"We sit there, eating in silence, and soon a faint light begins seeping through the window. The little kerosene lamp is put out to save what kerosene we have left. Then, as daylight comes, the cabin and the men emerge from the dark. The ceiling and half the walls are covered by a thick layer of hoarfrost, and as the stove heats up the room, the frost begins to drip. Little puddles form, on the table, in the beds, and on the floor. The floor is mostly covered with reindeer skins, but the cold comes through all the same and gathers round our feet.

"We are sitting by our coffee cups now, genuine coffee, letting a feeling of well-being spread through us. We have our regular seats. I sit at the end of the table with my back to the kitchen counter. The only one who smokes, I light my pipe. Next to me sits Arne Kjelstrup. He has a red beard, but his face is grimy. He has stomach trouble these days and keeps running outdoors at night. Then comes Claus Helberg. He is still crunching on bones. Einar Skinnarland, who escaped from the Gestapo and joined us in the mountains soon after his brother Torstein was arrested, is the last one at the long end of the table. It was he who supplied us with coffee, and now he is smiling broadly as usual. Only he is a bit disfigured, since he broke a front tooth the other day. Both he and Claus have long, unruly hair and beards. At the other end of the table sits Knut Haugland, looking civilized and well groomed, only a little down on his upper lip.

"Einar and I make a quick trip outside and stand there for a minute by the chopping block and sawhorse. The snow is bloodstained. A few reindeer skins and some heads and horns are scattered about. In the snowdrift on the south side of the cabin is some meat, more or less drifted over. West of the cabin, a little farther away, stands a marking pole. This is where most of the meat is dug down in the snow. The outhouse and garbage heap are right by the eastern gable wall, but we don't always make it that far when the wind and snow-drifting are at their worst.

"The weather where we are is fine, but in the Vrasjo mountains in the northwest some dark clouds are hanging.

" 'Storm clouds in the west,' Einar says as we go back inside, shivering with cold. 'No Gunnerside operation today.'

"From long and bitter experience, we have learned that as long as there are storm clouds over the Vrasjo mountains, there will be no attempt to land the Gunnerside men and their supplies by parachute. The flying weather is probably even worse farther west.

"We prepare ourselves for our day's work. Claus is going reindeer hunting again. Arne is going out to look for wood. Einar is to help Knut with the radio transmission. Myself, I start the day's work as a cook, and soon it is time to think of dinner. A new day has begun at the Cousin's Cabin, a day like so many others."

8 For the Gunnerside men, ready and waiting in Scotland to join their comrades on Hardanger Plateau, each day brought with it the same frustration. After being told in the morning to be ready to leave on the mission that evening, they would begin building up to the moment of departure. But just before sundown, a polite supervisor would unfailingly appear to tell them that because of weather conditions the order had been canceled. Finally, on January 23, 1943, during the moon period, when they were told to be ready again, the polite supervisor did not appear. They were taken in cars to an airfield used only for secret undertakings, where even the field personnel acted with the quiet circumspection of spies at work. Curious eyes were nevertheless raised at the sight of six heavily armed soldiers trudging through the rain in white camouflage suits with parachutes on their backs. Leif Tronstad, who had been made a colonel in the Royal Norwegian Army, was there to see them off.

"I cannot tell you why this mission is so important," he said to them, "but if you succeed, it will live in Norway's memory for a hundred years. Do your best, and good luck."

They had already been warned that they could expect no better treatment from the Germans than had been shown the glider troops, and now, right there on the airfield, each man was given his suicide capsule—a small, hermetically sealed rubber vessel containing a poisonous compound. It was said that if one were unlucky enough to swallow it whole, it would go right through the digestive tract without doing any harm, but that if one bit into it, death would come in five seconds.

A spy in civilian clothes usually has it sewn in the collar or lapel of his jacket, where it can be got hold of quickly in an emergency. But Rönneberg and his men were in British battle dress, with white skiing suits on top. It was a struggle just to slip the capsule down into the thigh pocket with the emergency bandage. How long would it take them, in a tight situation, to dig down through all that clothing and then get it into their mouths?

After handshakes and good-byes, they boarded a Halifax bomber and waited in silence as it taxied to the end of a runway and turned to windward. Wings, fuselage, and tail began to shake as the motors were revved up to take-off speed. Suddenly the long conelike structure, its brakes released, sprang forward, moving like a truck at first, then like a speeding car, then, as more and more air passed under the wings, like a racing car. The men sat staring down at their hands, their awareness of speed heightened by the fact that they could imagine, but could not see, the runway racing past. At the last and crucial moment before lift-off, they could actually feel the weight of the plane shift from wheels to wings.

Flying at an altitude of 10,000 feet, they crossed the North Sea to Norway's coastal belt, where breaking billows of surf looked like bursts of flowers in the moonlight. They remained at that altitude until they had crossed the first tier of mountains, then descended rapidly, setting course along the valleys to avoid being tracked by German radar stations. Taking turns at the one tiny peephole that gave them a view downward, they saw the snow-filled forests and ice-free fjords below, the frozen lakes and rivers and rolling white hills they had talked about during their long wait in Britain. They spotted upside-down boats beside inlets and streams, pointed out farms and homes, and even saw people looking upward as they roared past.

But clouds blew in before they reached their dropping place, and they could not see the red lights that Poulsson and his men, shivering in a fierce sub-zero wind, had laid out for them, in the shape of an L, on the ground. Poulsson was just returning to the landing site, after warming himself for a few minutes in the

Cousin's Cabin, when he heard the drone of a plane. Quickly flicking on a powerful white flashlight to contrast with the red lights on the ground, he aimed it at the invisible plane preceding the drone.

So they've come, after all, he thought, sucking on his empty pipe. They must have brought plenty of cigarettes and tobacco with them.

He kept looking upward, waiting for the Gunnerside party to float down out of the clouds, but nothing happened. The plane banked toward the west, its hum fading away behind the Grasdals mountain range. Poulsson kept the red lights on for another half hour in the hope that they would try again. Unfortunately, the pilot, unable to see the lights, decided at the last moment, while the plane was almost directly over the dropping place, to return to Scotland.

"It was very frustrating," Rönneberg later said, "to have to return, cold and stiff, to the same airfield we had left."

It was frustrating, too, for Tronstad, who was much more aware of the pressure being exerted by both London and Washington to get the mission launched. The success of the uranium pile in Chicago, coupled with the belief it engendered among the Allies that the Germans were far ahead in the race for an atom bomb, only added to that pressure. In fact, at the instigation of General Groves, the matter had already been brought to the attention of General Dwight Eisenhower, commander of American forces in Europe, who was told that the Vemork works had to be put out of commission at all costs—either by sabotage or by a massive air raid. Even Rönneberg and his men, who had never heard of Groves, began to feel the pressure. They could see it building up in Tronstad's face, as one cancellation of orders followed another and the abominable weather conditions continued.

"When we were brought back to Britain after the first failure to parachute out," Rönneberg said, "it was decided that it would be much better if we made a blind drop the next time. We would parachute out and find our way to Poulsson and his men on our own."

At long last, at one o'clock in the morning on February 17, during the full moon, they parachuted out onto Hardanger Plateau in an area where long, low, snow-clad hills looked like dunes built up by the wind.

"Do you know where we are?" Rönneberg asked Haukelid, who knew the plateau better than anyone else in the party.

"We may be in China, for all I know," Haukelid answered.

Because the latest intelligence of enemy dispositions had made it imperative that the aircraft avoid flying over Rjukan or the Mös dam, the dropping point had been changed at the last moment. Instead of parachuting near the Cousin's Cabin, as planned, they were to be dropped thirty miles to the northwest of Poulsson and his men, onto or near the frozen surface of Lake Skryken.

"It was obvious that we had not landed on the lake," Rönneberg said, "or even on the lake's shore. But we didn't have time to worry about that. We had to gather our equipment and stow it away before daylight."

Hans Storhaug, by far the best skier in the group, was the first to put on skis, and he soon came back with the warming news that there was a cabin about a mile away. This spurred the men on; they branched out in every direction in search of their equipment, dragged it all back, and stored it in a depot in the snow. After carefully marking the depot with stakes on which compass bearings were taken, they hurried to the cabin and jimmied the doorframe with an ax.

"Just getting in out of the wind was enough," Rönneberg said, "but it was a large, sturdy cabin, and piled near the stove was half a cord of birch wood."

The next day, after packing everything they needed for the sabotage operation and caching the rest away in the depot for pickup during their escape, they started out on skis to join Poulsson's group. Skiing conditions were almost perfect, but it had started blowing, and after traveling only about four miles they were assaulted from the rear by snow-laden gusts of wind that drove them onward, toward what they thought was their destination, but away from the protection of the cabin they had just left. They nevertheless continued on course, knowing how variable the weather is in Norway in winter. The farmers around the edges of Hardanger Plateau even have a saying about it: "If you don't like the weather, wait a minute."

Rönneberg was troubled, though, by something else. They were traveling in a direction based on the assumption that they had been dropped in the right place. But what if they had been dropped in the wrong place?

"What started my suspicion," Rönneberg said, "was that if we had been dropped in the right place, we should be going over a lake. It should therefore be flat, despite the swirling, wind-swept snow.

"But then we came upon a hump, and I saw bushes. Are they loose or fixed? I asked myself. If they're fixed, this isn't a lake and we're in the wrong place. I grabbed and pulled at them, and they were fixed, all right. By then some of the men were in a pretty bad way. We had spent months at sea level in the comparative warmth of Scotland, and now we were up over 3,000 feet on Hardanger Plateau in sub-zero temperatures. The sudden change of climate brought on something like muscular fatigue. We felt disoriented and feverish, the glands in our necks began to swell, and meanwhile the snowfall was thickening and the wind increasing. A storm was obviously on its way, and we were not even sure we were traveling in the right direction. There was nothing to do but return to the cabin and await developments."

With the pugnacious wind robbing them of breath, and the snowflakes flying like things with wings around them, they now had to find the cabin all over again. Not only had the new snow completely obliterated their ski tracks, but it had also made everything in the landscape look the same.

"How we managed to find the cabin, I don't know," Rönneberg said. "The truth is, we didn't find it; we more or less ran blindly into it."

By the time they opened the door and entered, snow coated their boots, ski outfits, and balaclava helmets; their faces were nearly frozen; they could hardly bend their stiffened legs. From around their eyes they removed hard, painfully clinging clumps of snow, and with their hands cupped over their noses and mouths they tried with the warmth of their breath to melt the frost that had formed in their nostrils. While doing these things, they could not help taking in, with their eyes and ears, the thunderous pounding of the storm, which created the strange sensation, perhaps because the cabin's only window was on its lee side, that they were tucked in behind a waterfall.

"The problem now was to find out where we were," Rönneberg continued. "There was a map on the cabin wall, and I started by making circles on it from the spot where we should have been. After completing the third circle, I found a dirty patch on the map —an area that had obviously been fingered often.

"On the chance that this fingered area was where the cabin was located, we decided to break into the cabin's other room. There, in a cupboard, we found a logbook, giving us the cabin's position. The greasy spot on the map was exactly where the cabin was located."

They decided to leave to join the advance party after the storm ended. Meanwhile, they would build a fire, eat, sleep, and dry their clothes. By daybreak the weather should be clear and the skiing conditions excellent.

But that night, with every mile of passage across Hardanger Plateau, the wind increased in velocity. It had obviously come on a long journey and was being fed an enormous amount of moisture, and now, as it rode up the coastal belt of mountains to the west, swirling upward into the colder atmosphere, it was disgorging that moisture in the form of snow—snow so thick and blinding that even with a searchlight they would not have been able to see a foot beyond the window.

The next morning, as the temperature dropped to five and ten below zero, the men prayed for a shift in the storm track. Iron-cold blasts of snow hit them as they piled out of the cabin to see what had happened while they slept. Already over twenty inches had fallen, and against the cabin and shed the drifts were twice that high. The storm was an all-engulfing reality, with fifty-mile-an-hour winds ripping the very fabric of air around them, jarring the shed, throwing snow against every prominence and curvature in the land. The wind alone made it hard to remember what they had come to Norway for, let alone to think they might succeed. There was a sense of being in the midst of something having prodigious weight and volume but no form, of being utterly unable to utilize past experience. The sheer fluid vastness of the storm absorbed them to the point where everything else shrank to insignificance. Some gusts of wind lasted so long, and reached points of such unremitting intensity, that they seemed incompatible with fixity itself.

"The cabin seemed about to be lifted," Rönneberg said, "even with all six of us, over half a ton of weight, inside."

That afternoon, when a chimney brace broke and he climbed on the roof to fix it, the blizzard took on still another dimension, if only because he was now literally surrounded by it under the sky. Like feathers, the snowflakes filled the atmosphere so thickly that the sense of an atmosphere was lost. As if inundated in some kind of wildly churning whiteness, he opened his eyes just a crack, with the muscles tensed, but there was nothing to see. The snow-laden wind blinded him and ripped his breath away; he had to feel for the brace, then bring its loose end back to where it belonged, while clinging to the other brace and playing one leg against the other in an effort not to slip. There were terrible impacts of snow and jarrings of air, vicious rushes of wind in which all the atmosphere seemed concentrated, and, above the steady roar, rending shrieks, like air-raid sirens. It was one continuous struggle against being blinded and suffocated, against a wind that rushed at the roof in wild, beseeching charges, one after another, without cessation. Screeching wind and howling wind, roaring wind and wind so tumultuous and excessive that at its highest pitch it seemed to express an aspiration to peace. Even in an earthquake there is the ultimate and final stability of earth. In such a storm as this there is no stability; everything moves, bends, breaks, or gives with the formless power of a wind whose roar alone sends the imagination reeling back to the wild beginning of life on this planet.

Suddenly, a vicious gust struck like a solid mass and lifted him bodily from the roof. For a second he found himself poised on a blast of air, before being thrown ten yards away into a heap of snow, as though he were a ball. When he tried to get up, he fell and was rolled over and over, as though he were being kicked and stomped by some concentrated part of the storm that had somehow focused on him. He felt himself joining the violence around him as he struggled and fought against it. Where was the cabin? He knew it could not be far away, but he could not see his own hand, much less anything as far away as ten feet. Using the wind as a guide, the same wind that had thrown him from the roof, he struggled against it, with his hands out, feeling his way like a blind man, until he came to the cabin wall and made his way round to the door.

By the next day, it was as if Hardanger Plateau had become the focus of the wind's activity, as if the center of the storm, constantly being fed new air as it unleashed the old, was content to remain where it was indefinitely. Every hour more snow fell; in whirls and rushes it piled up against the side of the cabin until it reached the roof. They had seen snow before, but never like this, never in such man-minimizing accumulations. And so it went all that night and into the third day.

"All hands," wrote Rönneberg in his log, "were filled with a great lassitude and weariness. The two who had been suffering from colds were now seriously ill."

The blizzard was so far beyond anything they had ever experienced that it began to take on an element of make-believe. There were times, outside the cabin, when nothing was stable for either feet or eyes to fix upon, and other times, during more tranquil periods, when the roll of the land took on an almost dreamlike quality. It was as if they were in their own little dell of solitude in a world composed of snow—of snow falling, snow accumulating, snow twisting from one place to another.

On the fifth day, without warning, the currents and whirlpools in the ocean of air above them underwent a dramatic change. The sky turned a turquoise blue; the wind died down; a cold hush lay over the snow-softened contours of the land. As in a dream, there was everywhere a monstrous kind of harmony between the vast accumulation of snow and what the wind had done to it. Gibraltarlike formations of rock looked like icebergs locked in seas of white. Cliffs were plastered with snow, and high up at the crests of some of them, enormous clumps of snow jutted out on the lee side, where the wind-frenzied flakes had consolidated with one another. Like huge, pendulous white noses, these clumps of snow reached out into space, their tons of weight held there by the power of their own cohesion.

Higher up in the mountains themselves, pinnacles and peaks and steeple-sharp crags were everywhere thickly crusted with snow, their jagged edges supporting hundreds of icicles from the freakish hours during the storm when the sun had shone long enough to start the snow melting. They looked like unevenly burned white candles, these crooked bits of rock in the sky—tall and serene and somehow, so exposed had they been to the storm, deserving of admiration. Like the cliffs and the ship-size rocks that rode the plains, these pinnacles and peaks were still recognizable as such. But everywhere else on the vast and desolate plateau, there was just the unaccented snow itself, which made the place something like another planet.

"I was afraid that Poulsson's party thought the storm had destroyed us," Rönneberg said later. "London had long since informed them of our successful parachute drop, and they had no way of knowing that we had found a cabin. We had to start out and join them as soon as possible, but first we had to get more food from our depot in the snow. We had taken just enough to carry out the mission, and we had eaten that during the five-day storm."

After searching a baffling network of snowdrifts a mile from the cabin, they found their cross-markings, dug down for fresh supplies, and skied back to the cabin to pack it in rucksacks for the trip. They were just about to leave when they saw a man, on skis and dragging a sledge behind him, about 200 yards away. Just seeing him there, absolutely alone, where everything permanent and fixed had been given a flowing form by the snow, was like witnessing a miracle. Where could he have come from, so soon after such a storm? They could not have been more surprised if he had emerged from the earth or dropped from the sky. And yet, as he left his sledge and started toward the cabin, he gave every indication of belonging to the area, of being calmly himself, preoccupied and engaged, like a man doing something habitual, natural, and necessary. There was a heedless kind of grace in the way he moved on skis, as though the muscles of his legs and the contours of the land were somehow currying each other's favor. He did not seem to be thinking at all of what he was doing, in fact, as he came closer and closer to what he obviously believed, or, rather, "knew," was an empty cabin. This only added to the peculiar kind of intimacy the men felt in relation to him, this man who seemed by the rhythm of his movements alone to be presenting his inmost self for their inspection.

But then he looked puzzled and started glancing quickly from the ski tracks he had made to the ones he could not have made— the ones around the trodden area outside the cabin door. He could

not believe and yet had to believe, or at least suspect, that someone was inside the cabin waiting for him. This should have lessened
his shock at being suddenly surrounded by six armed, bearded
men in uniform, but it did not. So convinced had he been of his
solitude and isolation that terror seized him. He threw up his
hands and fell to the ground.

"We calmed him down and brought him inside," Rönneberg
said. "He gave his name as Kristian Kristiansen and said he was
from Uvdal, a valley town along the northeast fringes of Hardanger
Plateau."

When they searched him, they found a wallet containing 3,000
Norwegian crowns, bread cards issued in Uvdal, and an identity
card showing that he did come from that town.

"What are you doing in the mountains?" Rönneberg asked.

"Hunting reindeer," Kristiansen said. "I have one young
female on my sledge out there."

After a few more questions, he admitted he sold the reindeer
meat on the black market, and he had a list of his customers to
prove it.

"Are you a member of the Quisling party?" Rönneberg asked.

Kristiansen hesitated, glancing from one soldier to another.
A simple man, who knew little about military life, and even less
about military uniforms, he obviously thought they were German
soldiers. Who else would dare wear military uniforms in Nazi-
occupied Norway?

"Well," he said, "I'm not exactly a member, but I support
that party."

"You support the Quisling party? Are you quite sure?"

"Yes. I am known as a supporter, but I still haven't gotten
around to joining."

Rönneberg and the others stepped outside to discuss what to
do with him. Since he had admitted he was a Quisling, there was a
strong feeling among some of the men that he should be shot.
Kasper Idland, who had no expectation of escaping to Sweden

after the operation, but who wanted the operation to be a success, offered to kill the Quisling himself.

"If you don't want to shoot him," he told Rönneberg, "I'll do it."

But on the chance that Kristiansen was just saying he was a Quisling in the belief that they were Germans, they decided to return to the cabin and put him to a test.

"Would your neighbors in Uvdal confirm your statement that you have Nazi sympathies?" he was asked. "Uvdal is not that far away. Your story can be checked out very quickly."

"I have so many enemies down there, I wouldn't be surprised if they said I was an anti-Nazi. You know, to get me in even deeper trouble."

This made it clear that Kristiansen thought they were German soldiers and was merely trying, in the time-honored way of people in occupied countries everywhere, to talk his way out of trouble. They spent several minutes trying to convince him that they, too, were Norwegians, but the man thought it was another trap, until someone said something in dialect about King Haakon.

At that he burst out himself in dialect: "God, but it's great to see you fellows. Here on the plateau, of all places!"

He waited, his eyes filled with a mixture of anticipatory joy at the thought that they might really be Norwegian and fear that he might have fallen into another trap. "I really am a Nazi. *Heil Hitler!*" he was prepared to say if they turned out to be German soldiers. But when they stopped questioning him, they all, finally, became Norwegian.

"You are quite safe if you do as we tell you," Rönneberg said to him. "We are not Nazis, not Germans. I take it that you are looking for an opportunity to help your king, that you have done nothing against him."

"Never. Not once."

Rönneberg, in recalling the incident, said, "Kristiansen was a very simple man, but to be on the safe side, I had him make out all the details of his black-market business, including a list of his customers, and sign his name to it, so we would have some assurance that he would not betray us.

"All the same, not killing him made things very difficult, because we knew we would have to let him go before we attacked the Vemork plant. We could not take his skis and rifle from him; they were his only means of survival. Nor could we lock him up in some cabin with only a few days' food supply. On the other hand, when we did let him go, after we joined up with Poulsson's party, would he have time to report us to the Germans in Uvdal before we were able to carry out the mission? It was a sticky question, one we still had not resolved, and meanwhile, we decided to make use of his knowledge of the area, since we had to keep him with us anyway."

Late that night, in the light of the moon, they loaded their sledge with explosives and supplies, told Kristiansen to leave his sledge behind, and started out. All six carried sixty-five-pound rucksacks on their backs and took turns pulling the sledge, with its 250-pound load.

"Kristiansen led the way, acting as scout," Rönneberg said. "He knew he had no choice—we had his rifle and list of black-market customers—so he took us along an excellent route. I still have visions of his amazing skill on skis, how he could crisscross his way up a hill, using every contour of the land to his advantage. I have thought of him many times since, of the smooth, seemingly thoughtless ability of that simple man in the mountains."

By daybreak they had reached the small, flat-roofed cabin that Kristiansen had stayed in during the storm. It belonged, he said, to his brother-in-law. There they decided to expend a little of their precious paraffin on a hot breakfast: oatmeal, powdered eggs, canned milk, and real coffee made with snow water.

After starting out again, they saw signs everywhere that reindeer had migrated into the area. A few large herds were actually sighted by Kristiansen, who was clearly disappointed at not being able to stalk them. His trained eyes saw everything there was to see, and it was while they were gliding down a slope leading to the Grasdalen that he raised his hand to alert the men behind him. Coming up the valley were two men on skis, one about 200 yards behind the other. Kristiansen had no idea who they were. When Rönneberg and his men flung themselves behind boulders and got their guns ready, he was again seized with terror at becoming involved in the war, here in the mountains, where until yesterday there had been no sign or hint of war.

When they went so far as to take his skis from him, to prevent any escape attempt in the event shooting broke out, his terror became almost uncontrollable. Down in Uvdal, where there were German soldiers and Norwegian civilians, he might have expected shooting. But up here in the wilderness, what was it all about? Trapped by events he neither understood nor had any power to control, he burrowed his way into the snow behind a boulder, wrapped his arms around his knees, and closed his eyes.

Rönneberg beckoned to Haukelid, his next in command, to come forward. Haukelid had trained in Scotland with Poulsson and the others of the advance party, so he knew them best.

"Do you recognize them?" Rönneberg asked, handing him a pair of binoculars.

The first skier was less than 300 yards away, well within the range of the binoculars. But he was so bundled up in clothing, his beard was so long and unkempt, and his helmet pulled so low around his ears and forehead that his own mother could not have recognized him.

"Put on your camouflage suit and civilian cap," Rönneberg said, "and go down and make contact with them. If they turn out to be strangers and start asking questions, just say you're a reindeer warden making your rounds. The rest of us will cover for you."

Haukelid unstrapped his rucksack, slipped on his camouflage

suit, and stuck his pistol in his belt beneath the suit. The two unknown skiers had by now passed by. When he skied up behind them, in the soft snow, careful to remain to windward of them, they neither saw nor heard him. Coming to a hillock just above and behind them, he leaned on his poles to study them a minute. They, too, had stopped, and were looking out over Hardanger Plateau through a telescope. It was one of those untarnished days that seem to exist only in high latitudes: the air was free of the slightest particle of dust; the sky appeared almost reachable; the plateau northward was so flat that the view seemed unlimited.

Could they be Claus Helberg and Arne Kjelstrup, out looking for the Gunnerside party after the storm? No. Impossible. They looked too ragged, too unkempt, too wan and thin. And yet their body builds—Helberg tall and slender, Kjelstrup medium height and broad—made Haukelid wonder.

Instead of calling to them, he gave a loud cough. They swung about, their hands on their guns, their eyes wide. Haukelid, too, had his gun in hand, for they had all trained at the same "Gangster School" in Britain. Then came a shock of recognition, smiles of delight, laughter, and shouts of joy.

"We kept waiting behind the boulders, our hands near our holsters," Rönneberg said later. "Then suddenly, above the noise of the wind, there were these wild yells of pleasure. We had at last joined with the advance party and could now prepare for the attack."

Though they were only about six miles from the Cousin's Cabin, they offered Helberg and Kjelstrup some of the delicacies in their rucksacks before taking off. They still had some crisp bread, and that was something the two men had not seen, let alone tasted, for months. There was powdered milk, which easily mixed with snow in a tin cup, dried fruit, raisins, chocolate, and tobacco, all imported from England, by plane, no less, only six days before.

Kristiansen, lost without skis, though obviously relieved that the two skiers were friends and not enemies of the soldiers, remained to one side.

"We again discussed the problem of what to do with him," Rönneberg said. "We could not leave anyone behind to guard him while we carried out the attack, and we could not lock him up to starve. Despite Idland's objections, we decided to set him free, under the threat that the information we had on him—his rifle, which was strictly forbidden, his black-market list, which would implicate his customers, and his assistance to us—meant that the Gestapo would kill him if he divulged any information.

"Still, we kept him with us for a while after we set out to join Poulsson and the others at the Cousin's Cabin, just to shorten the time between releasing him and carrying out the attack. Finally, I gave him rations for a week, an extra hundred crowns, and some English chocolate, an unheard-of luxury at that time in Norway. I told him he could not return to Uvdal for three days. He could resume his hunting if he wished, and stay as long as he wanted in the mountains, but when he did return he was to say nothing about what had happened, absolutely nothing, to anyone."

In the back of everyone's mind, as he moved away on skis in that unconsciously expert way of his, was whether they or Idland would prove to be right. Tronstad and Wilson had told them over and over again not to jeopardize the mission in any way. Should they have been ruthless and killed the reindeer hunter? Or should they have been true to their Norwegian instincts and let him go?

9 The reunion at the Cousin's Cabin that evening was wild and loud, with everybody trying to talk at once. At first the Gunnerside men were taken aback at the sight of so much blood on the snow around the chopping block, the scattered reindeer horns and hoofs, and at the way Poulsson and the others in the advance party devoured the greasy reindeer meat they had in a kettle on the stove. Organs, stomach contents, eyes, brains, and fat—everything went into their mouths with an abandon and relish that said more about what they had been through than words possibly could have. But it was not long before newcomers and old hands were sharing everything there was to share, especially the dehydrated fruits, vegetables, chocolate, and cigarettes the newcomers had brought with them. Poulsson, the one confirmed lover of tobacco in the group, began to chain smoke. He would use his pipe when the cigarettes ran out.

They slept in sleeping bags in cramped positions that night, all in the same room, some on beds and some on reindeer skins on the floor. The next morning, after a breakfast consisting of Norwegian venison and British cereal, canned milk, and coffee, the men crowded round the rugged pine table to discuss their planned attack on the heavy-water plant, some eighteen miles away. They turned to Joachim Rönneberg, the mission's leader, whose face took on a certain stringency of expression, as though serious discussion now might bring about the desired results later. He started by assigning each man his duty. Knut Haugland and Einar Skinnarland had already left for another cabin, at Skårbu, where they were to retain contact with London and report the results of the operation. Of the nine men left, four would be in the demolition party, and five in the covering party.

"The demolition party will consist of Fredrik Kayser, Birger Strömsheim, Kasper Idland, and myself," Rönneberg said. "The covering party will be led by Knut Haukelid, and will include Jens Poulsson, Claus Helberg, Arne Kjelstrup, and Hans Storhaug." He then gave a brief summary of the situation.

The target, the Vemork hydro plant, which includes several buildings as well as a hydroelectric power plant, stands like a fortress on a spacious shelf of rock blasted out of an almost vertical mountainside. So sheer is the drop from this shelf of rock that a stone pushed off the edge will fall 600 feet, without obstruction, until it hits the water or ice of the Måne River, flowing through the gorge below. Above the plant, the mountainside rises almost, but not quite, as steeply to a height of 3,000 feet, where canals, dams, and lakes feed water to twelve huge penstocks that carry it down to the power plant's turbines. All the buildings are situated at about the halfway mark between the top of the mountain and the gorge below, which is itself over a quarter of a mile above sea level. There are only three ways to reach the shelf of rock on which the buildings stand: the first is a narrow suspension bridge leading to it from the opposite side of the gorge; the second is a series of steps leading from the top of the mountain down along the penstocks to the roof of the power plant; the third is a single-track railroad running along a ledge hewn out of the rocky mountainside directly into the plant's yard. If a medieval king had searched all of Norway for an impregnable place to build a castle, he could not have found anything better than the shelf of rock on which the Norsk Hydro plant stands.

Since the penstocks and the plant were on the southern side of the valley, the likeliest approach was from the mountains on that side. But the Germans, anticipating an attack from that direction, had mined the entire area around the feed waters entering the penstocks. They had also placed machine-gun batteries at the valve house at the upper end of the penstocks and installed booby traps and all sorts of trip wires along the steps leading down the mountainside beside the penstocks themselves. The mountainside everywhere else was a sheer drop down into the gorge below.

"This rules out an approach to the plant from the mountains on the southern side of the valley," Rönneberg said. "We must make our approach from the northern side, where we are now. This means we'll have to cross the deep gorge that separates us from the plant. But before we get to that problem, or while we're thinking about it, let's get a better picture of the plant itself."

With pad and pencil, he proceeded to make drawings of the plant and the area surrounding it. He knew the layout better than anyone else because he had been briefed in London by Tronstad, who had planned and, with Jomar Brun, helped build the heavy-water plant that was now marked for destruction.

Remembering the Brun sketches that Tronstad had shown him, Rönneberg drew a diagram that showed the exact location of the high-concentration plant in the basement of the building, the steel door leading to the basement, the steel door leading to the ground floor, and the approaches to the plant itself, including the single-track railway that had been cut out of the mountainside on the plant's side of the gorge.

"These railway tracks are used only occasionally, for transporting machinery and equipment to and from the plant," Rönneberg said. "They extend right into the plant's yard, after passing beneath an iron-barred gate in the fence that surrounds the plant."

He then drew a small rectangle beside the large square representing the electrolysis building. "There is a barracks here," he said, "housing fifteen German soldiers. And over here, in the yard twenty yards away from the barracks, are storage tanks that will give us full firing range if we are detected."

On the chance that he might be killed before the objective was reached, Rönneberg then indicated the alternative entrance into the plant—the cable duct that Brun had pointed out to Tronstad in one of the sketches he had made of the plant during the planning of the operation in London.

"I am told that very few people even at Vemork know about this cable duct," Rönneberg said. "There is just enough space for one man at a time to crawl through, but we'll use it if we have to. It leads into a room in the basement right next to the high-concentration plant."

He put the pencil down and paused a moment. It was hard to be honest about the mission's chances without being grim as well.

"As you all know," he went on, "our main problem is the approach itself. We have all the necessary equipment and explosives to do the job, but we must reach the target to get the job done. Besides German sentries, we will have to avoid possible land mines. Then there are the natural obstacles that make the plant almost inaccessible except to those with passes to cross the suspension bridge over the gorge to the mountain ledge on which the plant is built. In short, our main problem is how to get onto that ledge, then into the plant itself, then back out again alive."

At this point everybody turned to Claus Helberg, a native of Rjukan and the man who had made several trips to the valley to reconnoiter the target area. "As I see it, we have two alternative approaches," Helberg said. "One is the narrow, seventy-five-foot suspension bridge at Vemork, where the rocky sides of the gorge are almost perpendicular. The other is to try to cross the gorge beneath the bridge, climb the cliff to the railway tracks on the other side, and follow the tracks into the plant unseen. We know the Germans don't expect anyone to try that route, because the gorge itself is not patrolled."

Jens Poulsson, another native of Rjukan, asked, "Why do we have to cross the gorge at that point? There may be a better place, farther down from the bridge, closer to Rjukan."

"Is the railway line from Rjukan to the plant guarded?" Rönneberg asked Helberg.

"According to my information, it is not guarded. But security measures have been tightened."

"We will have to find out before we decide on our approach," Rönneberg said. "Are the railway tracks mined?"

"They may have been recently. But it's unlikely, since the Germans don't expect anyone to attempt crossing the gorge."

"What about the fence around the plant?"

"The Germans have increased the height of the barbed-wire fence, but the gate where the tracks pass can be opened with steel cutters."

"If the railway is not guarded, then," Rönneberg said, "and they haven't mined it, it is the one weak point in the defense system around the plant. But German activities in the area are in a state of flux. Changes are apparently being made from day to day. We'll have to obtain completely current information before launching the attack."

"I have a friend in Rjukan who is at the plant every day," Helberg said. "He'll have all the up-to-date information we need."

The friend was Rolf Sörlie, the construction engineer at the plant. Sörlie had joined the resistance movement the year before, and Helberg knew he could be trusted. No one but Poulsson in the Gunnerside party had ever met Sörlie or heard his name, and Helberg, operating on the first principle of any agent, did not divulge his identity.

A plan was devised whereby Helberg would go down alone to the valley to meet his contact and rejoin the others in Fjösbudalen, in a cabin known to both Helberg and Poulsson.

"You can put your uniform on there, Claus, before the attack," Poulsson said.

Fjösbudalen is a small mountain area on the opposite side of the valley from Vemork, near where Hardanger Plateau dips down toward the Måne River and the rocky gorge it has cut during its thousand years' journey to the sea. The small cabin there would be their last and most advanced base before the attack.

"It will be unoccupied at this time of year," Poulsson said. "And it's close enough to Vemork to make our final approach short and simple."

Helberg, his clothing still bloody from all the reindeer hunting he had done since Christmas, changed into something more presentable and shaved his beard before he left. Knowing every turn in the trail, he took the most direct route to Gvepseborg, where a cable-car lift connects the top of the mountain with the Rjukan valley below. It was built by the Norwegians before the war for recreational purposes, to enable the people of Rjukan to enjoy the benefits of the sunlight during the four winter months when the rays of the sun fail to reach Rjukan's streets. The top station of the lift is called Gvepseborg, and the bottom station Krosso, and Helberg knew that once he decended to Krosso he would have no trouble finding Sörlie, who lived in the valley a short distance away.

Of course, the Germans had taken over control of the cable-car lift and discontinued the public's use of it for the duration. It was still in operation, though, and the man in charge of it, a Norwegian, lived in a house a short distance from the top station, where the controls were located. Helberg passed this house as quietly as possible and started down a steep, snow-clogged road, the Ryes Road, which crisscrosses its way down the mountainside beneath the cables stretched from the top to the bottom station. Built by workmen during the construction of the lift, this road was seldom if ever used in winter, and was used only by the hardiest mountain climbers in summer.

The day, February 25, happened to be Rolf Sörlie's brother's birthday, and there was a party in progress at the Sörlie house. Helberg and his friend got together in a nearby garage, where they discussed the German defense system around the plant and how it had been strengthened since the abortive glider attack.

"Helberg and I grew up in Rjukan," Sörlie said later, "and I think we both thought it more or less impossible to cross the gorge. During our meeting I don't remember that we discussed it seriously, and he didn't tell me it was being considered."

Afterward, to avoid being seen by anyone, Helberg spent the night in the garage, almost freezing to death despite the birthday-party food that Sörlie brought him. He set out again at dawn, but instead of returning up the Ryes Road, which was extremely steep, he skied along the valley highway toward the suspension bridge that led across the gorge to Vemork. This highway ran above, and parallel with, the gorge itself, and it was while he was skiing along, looking downward through the outcrops of pine and birch, that he "got the idea, or the impression, that it was possible for Gunnerside to cross the gorge and avoid shooting the guards on the bridge."

When he reached the unoccupied cabin in Fjösbudalen, he broke in and immediately began searching for something to eat. "The chocolate the Gunnerside men had brought from Britain had whetted my appetite for sweets," he recalled. "So I rushed to the cupboard, and there I found just what I was looking for—a tin of syrup. I smiled, got a spoon, and sat down by the window to enjoy it. But the tin had been insecurely sealed, and now the whole surface of the syrup was coated with dead ants. I sat there, torn between my desire for the syrup and my repugnance at the sight of the dead ants. In the end the ants won; they were too un-appetizingly visible to be ignored."

His comrades arrived later that day, with food and the paraffin to heat it. Helberg, his handsome bony face stamped with the knowledge he had gathered, waited until he got something hot inside him before getting down to business.

"Patrolling the suspension bridge are two German guards with Tommy guns," he began. "Their guardhouse, alongside the road leading up the hill from the bridge to the factory compound, is equipped with an alarm button. Machine guns and floodlights are mounted on top of the main building, and if the alarm is raised, the floodlights illuminate the entire area, including the penstocks above the building, the suspension bridge below the building, and the roads leading to and from the bridge. The German soldiers in the barracks just outside the building are also routed out, and the German garrison in Rjukan, only a few miles away, is alerted.

"But the gorge itself is not guarded, and neither is the railway leading directly into the plant's yard."

Kasper Idland, the one man in the party who was unsure of himself on skis, broke in at this point. "It still seems to me that the easiest and quickest approach is across the suspension bridge, after we silence the guards. From there we go up the steep slope to the railway, then due west along the railway to the fence. We cut through the fence and move into the factory yard between the power plant and the electrolysis plant."

Helberg and Poulsson disagreed. They said it would be impossible to cross the bridge without alerting every German garrison in the valley.

"Shooting the guards will create too much noise before we get inside the building, and perhaps even reduce our small contingent," Helberg said.

Rönneberg had air photographs of the Rjukan-Vemork area, as well as pictorial views, from Norwegian guidebooks, that had been taken in peacetime from the cable-car platform on top of the mountain diagonally across the valley from the Vemork plant. These photographs revealed that small trees and shrubs grew out of cracks in the rock wall leading down into the gorge on either side.

"Where trees grow," Rönneberg said, "a man can climb."

He passed the photographs around, and the men agreed. But the photographs had been taken in summer, and this was winter. It was hard to be sure—and they had to be sure. Therefore, the next morning Helberg got his skis on again, this time to go down and find out, once and for all, whether the gorge could be crossed.

"Be careful, and keep in mind the success of the mission," Rönneberg told him. "Nothing else counts. If we fail, an air bombardment of the plant will follow. Many Norwegian workers and civilians will be killed."

Helberg nodded and pushed off, raising a trail of powdery snow behind him as he sped down the slope leading southward from the cabin. With not a cloud in the sky, the sun's rays kept bouncing off the snowy surface into his eyes, especially when he had to dip and turn around jagged boulders sticking up like the prows of icebound ships. He had his pistol with him, and of course his suicide capsule, but he knew where the populated areas were and how to avoid them. As he went he kept making mental notes that would help him guide the men in the dark that night, during the approach. A turn here, a ridge there, then downward and eastward between the trees and brush.

When he came to the highway that led to Rjukan, he followed it on skis to where it started to make a long U curve downward around the mountainside. This U curve is almost half a mile long, and at the end of it, where the lower section of highway begins, there is a small hamlet called Våer. Since the attacking force would have to avoid this built-up area during the approach, he decided to test the route the men would be taking in the dark that night. Unfastening his skis, he left the highway and started climbing downward, through the brush, in a straight line that avoided the U curve altogether. The climb was difficult and precarious even in daylight, but he managed to keep going until he came to the lower section of highway at the end of the curve. Walking eastward toward Rjukan along this lower section, he kept looking downward through the trees and brush until he came to a place where he thought he could climb down the rest of the mountainside into the gorge below. At this point he took his skis and poles and climbed up above the highway through the brush to an abandoned road, the power-line road, which ran parallel to the highway and about thirty yards above it.

We can leave our skis and equipment here tonight, he thought. No one ever uses this road any more.

But first he had to find out whether the climb down into the gorge was possible, and the only way to do that was to climb down. Leaving his skis and poles behind, he slid through the snow back to the main road, crossed it, and started down through the brush below. Luckily, the snow had formed a surface crust hard enough to support him when he dug his boots into it. There were also rocky, ice-covered surfaces, though, and once he started down in a sudden, precipitous slide that might have resulted in a broken bone if it had not been for a well-placed juniper bush in the path of his descent. And several times he found himself hip deep in pockets of soft snow where it had accumulated on the shelves of rock. No doubt of it, without the juniper bushes and the branches of spruce and birch to cling to, this approach would have been out of the question.

After slipping and sliding downward a few more times, he found himself standing on the frozen river in the middle of the gorge, about a quarter of a mile from the suspension bridge. There was no wind and not a soul in sight, and for just a moment, with the mountains plunging upward thousands of feet on either side, he remembered the winters of his boyhood in Rjukan, when the sun's rays never reached the town. He and his classmates had a joke about it. "Let's walk on the sunny side of the street," they'd say. Then when April came and the sun rose higher in the sky, they always did walk on the sunny side.

Down here on the frozen river, he had a much better view of both sides of the gorge. He started walking east toward Rjukan, away from the suspension bridge. A bit farther down he saw a groove where a descent into the gorge would be less difficult than the one he had just made. Scraggy spruce and pine grew out of cracks in the rocks on either side of the groove, and even the incline appeared less steep.

After a few more minutes of searching, he found a similar groove on the other side, where they could çlimb up to the railway tracks leading into the hydro plant's yard. The climb would have to be made in the dark, though, with heavy packs of explosives, equipment, and guns. Still, anything was better than alerting the guards on the bridge and then having to fight their way into the factory itself.

Everything would depend on the weather. If it remained cold, they would have no trouble crossing the river. But if a foehn suddenly set in, with its warm air sweeping down the mountainside into the valley, the ice and snow would turn to slush, the river would rise with the sudden thaw, and the compressed air would become powerful enough to blow them out of any tree. During his childhood, one such foehn had blown a locomotive clear off its tracks, only two miles from Rjukan.

Against such a wind, the men would not be able to stand, let alone climb. They would be trapped in the valley—easy targets for alerted German guards.

10 "I found a place where we can climb down into the gorge," Helberg reported to the others. "I made the climb myself, right down to the river, so there's no doubt about it. There is also another place, not far away, where we can climb up the other side to the railroad tracks. I didn't climb up to the tracks, though, for fear of being seen from the highway. That climb will be more difficult, much more difficult, but it can be done."

The men saw the problem in different ways. Some agreed with Helberg that they should leave their skis and equipment on the power-line road above the highway and pick them up after they retreated back across the gorge. Rönneberg disagreed; he wanted a faster retreat, one that would take only seconds to cross the gorge —and that meant using the suspension bridge.

"I think we'll be trapped by the Germans in the valley if we try to go back the same way," he said. "After the sabotage, it will take time to cross the gorge again and climb back up the mountainside to pick up our skis and equipment on the power-line road. Even if we succeed in getting in and out of the plant undetected, the explosion will almost certainly alert the German soldiers in the barracks. They in turn will alert the German troops in Rjukan. We will be trapped in the valley if the troops get to the top of the mountain before we do."

"After the explosion," Helberg said, "the first thing the troops in Rjukan will do is rush to Vemork. By the time they get there, we'll be gone. Besides, when we get to the top of the mountain, we'll have skis. They won't."

Knut Haukelid, in command of the covering party, agreed with Rönneberg that they should use the suspension bridge to cross back over the river. Getting back up to Hardanger Plateau would be much faster that way, at a time when half a minute might mean the difference between escape and capture. The skis and equipment, Rönneberg and Haukelid felt, should be left up on top of the mountain, and only the arms, explosives, and a little food carried down the mountainside.

This was more in keeping with the original plan devised by Tronstad and Wilson in London.

"Besides," Poulsson added, his sharp features serious, "will we be able to climb the gorge twice in the same night? By the time we get back to our skis and equipment on the power-line road, we'll be exhausted. And then, in order to reach the top of the mountain and the possibility of escape, we'll still have 1,500 more feet to climb, through three feet of snow."

But Poulsson was a Rjukan man, and at all costs he wanted to protect the townfolk he had known since childhood.

"I am still against using the suspension bridge, though," he said, "because it would mean killing the German sentries. Even if we're able to kill them without suffering any casualties on our side, there will be severe reprisals against innocent people in Rjukan."

It was again Helberg, the improviser, who supplied an alternative. "We leave our skis and equipment where I originally suggested," he said, "on the power-line road above the highway. After the sabotage, we get back across the gorge as fast as possible and climb back up to the power-line road. Only now we don't go back the same way. We go along the power-line road in the opposite direction, *toward* Rjukan, until we come to the lower platform of the cable-car lift. A narrow mountain road zigzags its way clear up to the top of the mountain beneath the cable-car lift. It's called the Ryes Road. It was used when the cable lift was being built, and it's still in good condition. To go straight up the side of the mountain through three feet of wet snow would be almost impossible anyway, even if we did use the suspension bridge as an escape route after the explosion. We'd become separated before we made it to the top."

A decision had to be made, and Rönneberg, as the leader of the group, had the right to make it himself. Since Helberg and Poulsson were Rjukan men, they had probably zigzagged their way up the Ryes Road under the cable lift many times. But Rönneberg did not want to force his men to follow a dubious course. Fighting the Nazis, after all, was now their first calling in life; they each deserved to have a say.

"I asked each man individually, one at a time, how he felt about it," Rönneberg recalled. "I made it very democratic, because it was important to make everyone happy. That way, you have a more cohesive and co-operative unit."

When time came for Idland to express his opinion, he surprised everyone.

"I don't care which escape route we take," he said, "because I don't put much faith in the idea of escape. I don't expect to reach Sweden."

He had been told by his comrades that the retreat across Norway to Sweden would be difficult, if not impossible, without skis. This made success extremely dubious for him.

"Where there's life," Helberg said to cheer him up.

The vote on the escape route went in Helberg's favor; the majority sided with the home-town boys, Helberg and Poulsson, who knew the surrounding mountains better than anyone else.

"We retreat across the gorge, then," Rönneberg said. "Now let's get on with it. If all the steel doors leading into the building are locked, and the cable duct is blocked off, too, the demolition party will have to use explosives to blow the lock on one of the steel doors. In that case, the covering party will have to be ready for anything.

"Once in the high-concentration room with explosives, the demolition party should complete the operation in about seven minutes. Of course, something may happen to delay us, so the only sure signal the covering party will have that the job has been completed will be the sound of the explosion itself. By then, the demolition party should be back in the yard outside the building. The signal for withdrawal, as you all know, is 'Piccadilly?' And the answer, 'Leicester Square.'

"If anything should happen to me, or anything should upset the plan, everyone must act on his own with the goal in mind to complete the operation.

"We will carry our guns with the magazines filled, but with no cartridge in the chamber. Someone may trip and fall or pull the trigger out of nervousness, and we don't want any accidental firing to give us away to the German guards.

"If we are detected, though, and the alarm is sounded, the covering party will attack the German guards immediately. The demolition party will concentrate on getting inside the plant no matter what happens, but if the demolition party is killed before the plant is reached, the covering party will take over the placing of the explosives. In short, if fighting breaks out, everyone must act on his own initiative in order to complete the operation. Someone must arrive at the objective to do the job.

"We will leave here at eight o'clock tonight to give ourselves plenty of time to get there. Helberg will lead the way from here to our depot on the power-line road. After we leave our skis and equipment on the power-line road, he will lead the way down into the gorge and up to the railway track. There is a change of guard on the suspension bridge every two hours, at eight, ten, midnight, and so forth. We will begin our attack half an hour after midnight, to give the relieved guards a chance to relax and the fresh guards time to lose their initial alertness.

"As for our escape, you all have maps and compasses, and I urge you to study the details you will have to remember if things get tight.

"Finally, to repeat what we were all told in Britain, Hitler has ordered every saboteur or commando, whether in uniform or not, to be shot. So if any man is wounded, or about to be taken prisoner, he ends his own life."

For four months, while fighting for survival up on the Hardanger Plateau, Poulsson and his men had not given a thought to suicide, let alone to the capsules with which they had been supplied. Now that they were physically fit again and about to go on the mission, the capsule regained the same importance it had had when they had first left Britain.

Perhaps to relieve the tension that was building up, someone said, "What is heavy water, anyway? I mean, can you drink it? Does it look and taste like water?"

Some were surprised to learn that it did indeed look and taste like water, and was even harmless to drink. My God, then, is the mission worth the risk? Someone might have said that, but no one did.

They sat around checking their guns and filling their rucksacks with tins of food, compasses, flashlights, elastic bandages, chocolate, Chinese silk maps, medical preparations and bandages, extra bootlaces and gloves, and tiny saws for use if a frostbitten finger or toe had to be amputated. Poulsson pulled on cigarette after cigarette with even greater dedication than usual, as if in anticipation of the long hours in the dark during the mission when he would not be able to smoke at all. Others talked of rejoining their families after the war in the Norwegian towns where they had gone to school and learned to ski. Having no letters from home to read, though, and no photographs of loved ones to study, they expressed themselves in ambiguous ways. It was actually easier, now that they were back in Norway, with their home towns still occupied by the Germans and their mission about to start, to talk about going "home" to Britain.

"Joachim," Idland said in private to Rönneberg at one point during the tense hours of waiting, "when you told me in Scotland about this operation, I realized I didn't belong in the party, I am such a poor skier. But I felt it was too late to tell you about it. For one thing, there was only one week left before we were to leave for Norway. For another—and this was the most important reason—I was convinced I would have no difficulty in keeping up with the others until we reached the plant and got the job done. The retreat to Sweden didn't interest me. I don't think there's going to be a retreat. Tronstad was very honest with me in Scotland. He didn't put much faith in the idea of our escaping to Sweden either."

A man who does not expect to live can often, in a crisis, act in a way that precludes any chance of living. Idland was the man who had wanted to shoot Kristian Kristiansen, the black-market reindeer hunter, and the guards on the bridge, if necessary. It was almost as if he had set a time clock for his own death and now could not wait for the time to run out.

"You will not delay us during the attack," Rönneberg said firmly. "And you will not delay us during our retreat."

A few minutes later, one of those odd couplings of war and peace took place just outside the cabin. Helberg, Haukelid, Kjelstrup, and Storhaug were sitting in the sun on a log by the entrance cleaning their guns. Helberg, who had his own Colt .32 revolver for the mission, and a Tommy gun as well, was thinking of the route to which he had committed his comrades. Though convinced he had chosen the best one, he was worried about possible snags, especially during the retreat up the road under the cable-car lift. If they were detected and the Germans knew they were retreating up the Ryes Road, it would take only a matter of minutes to telephone the Norwegian operator at the top station and get the cable car going. German soldiers crowding into the lower-station car would reach the top of the mountain long before the Gunnerside men could possibly reach it on foot.

Suddenly, he was jolted out of his concentration by the sight of two young Norwegian couples, their skis over their shoulders, trudging hand in hand up the hill toward a neighboring cabin. They, too, were in their early twenties, and the girls were beautiful, with smooth, almost transparent skin and cheeks reddened by the frost. They saw Helberg and his companions at almost the same instant that Helberg and his companions saw them. Mutual surprise and wonder gave way to curiosity as the four young people, with discreet smiles, continued in silence toward the neighboring cabin, about thirty yards away. For the soldiers, just watching them was like being transported backward to time before the war, when the trains from Oslo and the buses from Konesberg were full of such couples, young and old, lovers all of life out of doors.

"I *know* one of the men," Helberg said. "His name is Kare Tangestad. Jens and I went to school with him. The three of us were in the same class."

The young lovers, with their sleeping bags and rucksacks of food, personified everything wonderful and true about Norway as it was before the German occupation. Why am I here, Helberg wondered, feeling as though his training in Britain, the uniform he was wearing, and the sabotage in which he was about to take part had somehow altered his identity.

This feeling of being out of place in time grew even stronger when he approached the two couples and Tangestad failed to recognize him.

"You know me?" Tangestad said.

"Yes," Helberg said. "Don't you know me?"

Tangestad looked more closely, hesitated a moment, and shook his head. This astonished Helberg, but after five grueling months in the mountains, during one of the worst winters on record, he did in fact look different. The monotony of those days of waiting, the weeks of illness he had endured, the sameness of face and food and the ravages of snow, wind, and freezing cold had made him older, thinner, grimier. Besides, he was in a British army uniform.

Poulsson had been more successful in withstanding the hardship in the mountains, and when he stepped from the cabin and joined the group, Tangestad remembered him, and then, finally,

Helberg, too. This intensified the young man's curiosity, and that of his companions. What were Norwegians in British battle dress doing in the middle of southern Norway almost three years after the beginning of the German occupation?

Helberg's and Poulsson's curiosity was equally intense. They were most anxious to talk to this classmate who had lived in their occupied home town during all the months since their escape. It was an experience that had been denied them and one they wanted to share. But exchanging reminiscences was out of the question, and little was said. When it became clear that the two couples intended to spend the night in the adjoining cabin, they were escorted to it and told by Poulsson that they would have to remain indoors until the following evening. He offered no explanation, and they asked for none.

After they closed the door behind them, it was not long before the snow helmeting the chimney of their cabin began to melt from the heat of the fire they had started inside. The melting snow and the chimney smoke rising up through the middle of it were the only signs of life, but for the soldiers, cleaning their weapons and waxing their skis, there was something detaining and poignant in the scene. With their extremely hazardous mission about to start, they appeared troubled by some kind of bad timing they could not identify, as though war and peace had become forms of each other in their minds.

11

The men had already destroyed everything of foreign origin that might betray them: empty raisin, cooky, milk, and ration tins, the wrappings of fruit, chocolate, and pemmican bars, used jars of frostbite ointments, all from Britain. While Rönneberg stood outside the cabin for a moment, they sat with that earnest-eager look found in college locker rooms before a game. Talk stopped like candles going out.

"All right, men," Rönneberg's deep voice said when he came back, "let's get going."

Filing out under clouds scudding low above them, they instinctively squinted into the wind as if in appraisal of its obscure source, its scope and hidden strength. Since sundown it had increased by at least fifteen miles an hour, and now it was picking snow off the ground and blowing it like picnic litter through the air. A storm was the one thing they did not need, but they said nothing as they fastened on their skis, strapped their rucksacks to their backs, and gripped their poles. Across the way, smoke was coiling from the chimney of the other cabin in the moonlight, but already they looked upon their encounter with the two young couples as something that might not actually have happened. It might have been only an apparition, it seemed so far removed from what they were about to do, or try to do. On Rönneberg's signal, they glided off toward the Rjukan valley, led by Claus Helberg, who had a feeling for movement and terrain, the sudden grace and uninterrupted reflexes of a deer, and the ability to sense rather than decide what to do in an emergency.

The first mile down the mountainside was steep and straight, and everyone behind Helberg followed at a good pace in his tracks. Then the woods thickened; they were forced to carry their skis and climb down through the brush, where the snow was deep and loose, and the surface of it moved with the wind around their legs. Using as a guide the telephone lines connecting the mountain above with the valley below, they rammed their way through thickets of shrubs and lopped-off branches of trees, sliding and wading downward from one telephone pole to another. Though they tried to keep close together, it was difficult and sometimes impossible. One man might find himself caught by a branch hidden beneath the snow, while another, taking a free and unexpected ride downward, went flying past him into the darkness below.

"Along the telephone line it was very difficult, steep country," Rönneberg said later. "We sank in the snow up to our waists."

Above them the telephone wires, sagging beneath a clinging load of snow, swayed back and forth in the increasing wind until the weight of the snow overcame its cohesive power. Then some of it dropped off, lessening the weight on the wires enough to make them vibrate. This dislodged more snow, which in turn made the wires vibrate again and dislodge still more snow.

The men, struggling under the fifty-pound weights of their rucksacks, hardly noticed these little showers of snow from the vibrating wires, but to Poulsson they signified the possible beginning of the dreaded foehn. He could feel the air growing warmer against his face as it swept in gusts down the flanks of the mountain into the valley below. If he was right, the ice on the river would melt, the river itself would rise with snow water, and the three feet of dry snow through which they were now trudging would turn to slush. After the operation, their escape across the gorge and back to Hardanger Plateau would be that much more difficult and hazardous.

When they reached the upper section of highway that Helberg had traveled in civilian clothes that afternoon, they put their skis back on and glided down it, along the edge, where the snow was still soft, with Helberg far out in front. Below the soft snow was the surface of the hard snow, which had fallen earlier and grown thick and icy by melting a little during the day and freezing at night. Digging their poles into this icy subsurface, they descended farther down into the valley, where the air kept getting warmer, the thaw more advanced, and the entire surface of the road more slippery.

"The road was as slippery as a skating rink," Helberg recalled. "Now and then the wind came in gusts so strong that we slipped and fell. But in one sense the weather could not have been better, for who but us would be out on such a night?"

Despite the wind, the chronic throbbing of the Vemork plant became audible as they continued downward. Then, in a sudden burst of moonlight, they saw the plant itself, far below them on the other side of the gorge. The huge seven-story electrolysis building, made from 800 tons of steel, 1,700 barrels of cement, and blocks of stone cut out of the mountain itself, stood in front of the power-house on a ledge of rock between the top of the mountain and the Måne River running through the gorge below. Rising 900 feet above the snow-covered roofs of these two main buildings were twelve penstocks, each with a diameter of five and a half feet, carrying endless tons of water from canals, dams, lakes, and reservoirs on top of the mountain down into the plant below. This constant flow of water—1,750 cubic feet every second, 105,000 cubic feet every minute, 6,300,000 cubic feet every hour—had melted the snow covering the penstocks, and they loomed even larger against the snow surrounding them and the plant they supplied. No fortress could have been more protected by nature, or better situated to withstand an assault. Only the single-track railway, running on a narrow shelf along the mountainside, and the slender suspension bridge crossing the moat-like gorge 300 feet above the river, gave access to it.

For everyone in the party it was an impressive sight, but for Jens Poulsson, who had not seen the Vemork plant since his escape from the German occupation forces in January 1941, it was a profoundly moving sight as well. He had escaped the Nazis by skiing across the mountains to Sweden, where he tried to fly to Britain to rejoin the remnants of the Royal Norwegian Army forming there. But no aircraft operated between Sweden and Britain in 1941, so he continued on through Finland and down through the Soviet Union to Turkey, in the hope of boarding a ship going through the Mediterranean and up along the Atlantic to Britain. With the Italians and Germans still dominating the Mediterranean, however, only warships could get through the Strait of Gibraltar. So from Turkey, Poulsson pushed on, through Syria, Lebanon, and Palestine, to Egypt, where he boarded a ship going through the Red and Arabian seas to India. From India he recrossed the Arabian Sea to the east coast of Africa and went down the African coast to Capetown, where he boarded a ship bound for Trinidad. From there he made his way by ship and plane to Canada, where he finally, after many delays, boarded a plane bound for Britain, arriving in October 1941, nine months after his escape from his German-occupied homeland.

Now, back in Norway, only a few miles from where he was born, and opposite the huge hydro plant he had watched being built while he was growing up, he was about to take part in a sabotage attempt against the plant. For a fleeting moment, the whole thing appeared as improbable as his long, circuitous trip from Norway to Britain.

When they came to where the highway made the long U curve down around the mountainside to the small hamlet called Våer, they again removed their skis, and, using gravity as well as strength, because of the steep grade, slipped and slithered downward through the brush, under a moon that shone in bits of open sky among the trees. Just as they reached the lower section of highway beyond Våer, two buses, carrying the Vemork night shift from Rjukan, came lumbering along, their headlights throwing beams of light into the woods where the road curved upward. The men, sliding and slipping through the wet snow above the road, dug in, grabbed branches, and used their poles in a desperate effort to retard their descent and avoid the light. As the last bus passed, one or two of the men barely missed landing on its roof.

With Helberg well ahead again as scout, they continued along the lower section of highway to where the power-line road ran above and parallel to it along the mountainside. Here Helberg led the way from the highway through the dark woods up to the spot on the power-line road where they were to hide their skis and rucksacks for pickup during their retreat. When they assembled, they smiled and nodded to one another in silence, their eyes gleaming with eagerness, fear, and hope, as though they all not only felt the same, but also had forgotten everything in their lives that made them different. Removing the white camouflage suits they had thus far worn over their British army uniforms, they packed them in their rucksacks for retrieval later. From this point on it would be a strictly military operation, carried out in uniform to avoid reprisals against the local civilian population.

The hum of the plant was louder in the warm, downward draft of air into the valley. They could hear the whirl and whirr of the dynamos, the commotion and tumult of gyrating machinery, and the plunge of water through the penstocks. The different sounds mingled and became something like the over-all sound of a nearby city. Somehow it seemed in tune with the commotion in their hearts, and as it closed in on them, so did the shared knowledge of what they were about to attempt.

"Birger," Rönneberg said to Strömsheim, who was in the demolition party, "you have your set of charges?"

Strömsheim, transferring packages of explosives, detonators, and fuses to a small, specially constructed rucksack for the climb across the gorge, nodded.

"Good," Rönneberg said, "and I have mine."

There were two complete sets of charges; Rönneberg had one and Strömsheim the other, "just in case anything should happen to either one of us," Rönneberg said later.

The others pocketed hand grenades, knives, a little food, and extra ammunition, and checked their Tommy guns and pistols. Kjelstrup, of the covering party, slung a pair of armorer's shears and some rope over his broad shoulder. Then they all hid their rucksacks, along with their skis and poles, in snowy beds of spruce and balsam needles. It was almost ten o'clock, and they still had to cross the gorge.

Rönneberg hesitated, and looked each man squarely in the eye, as though the mission's outcome depended upon how they looked back at him now.

"All right, let's go. Helberg leads the way."

Not another word was spoken. They knew what they were up against, so their determination was without the impetus of being blind. With their eyes wide open and their hearts pounding, they vanished, one by one, into the black abyss, swinging down through a sloping, concave groove in the rocks like bundles sliding down a ramp.

12 Down at the bottom of the gorge, the effects of the thaw were more noticeable. Water was trickling down the rock face into the remaining patches of snow, which turned spongy before melting into the squelchy earth. This created still more water, and as it spread inquiringly around the rocks by the river's edge, the ice on the river began to look like the deck of a slowly sinking ship. Where the ice had already split apart, it was no longer level.

"The river ice was about to break up," Rönneberg recalled. "There was only one usable 'bridge' left, with three inches of water on it."

First to cross was Claus Helberg, strangely comforted by the thought that there was a chance of slipping. He stepped nimbly, one foot here, one foot there, like someone playing hopscotch with both feet. The others followed, one by one, in order not to put too much weight on the ice at one time. But would the water-floored bridge of ice be here for their escape two hours from now? Though no one asked the question, it was on everyone's mind as the last man crossed.

This side of the gorge was much steeper. It represented the last natural obstacle between them and the target, and they all looked up in silence at the slants, angles, and shelves in the rock face and the bits of spruce and pine growing out of cracks and crevices. Each man would have to choose and test each hold for himself and then hope for the best. One mistake or misstep would mean death, or, worse, broken bones, for all around them were sharp, recently fallen rocks, not yet smoothed by the running river water.

A few of the men, as if trying to get a head start, reached up and got their fingers in cracks in the rock even before Rönneberg gave the order to climb. The others followed suit, making tentative judgments about the first holds they would use. Their climb down the mountainside into the gorge had developed their sense of touch in ways they neither understood nor questioned. They could tell the weight and strength now of anything they felt with their hands, tried with their feet, or leaned against with their bodies. The darkness had probably helped, just as blindness helps the blind to know and evaluate things by feeling them.

Rönneberg signaled "Go" with his hand, and, as he later recalled, "we started clambering up the sheer rock face toward the Vemork railway 600 feet above us."

Grabbing branches and ledges of rock, feeling with their feet for holes and crevices, they pulled themselves up to new positions, where they settled for a moment, listening to the drumming slosh of snow water pouring down grooves around them. The idea was to find a support for each foot and a hold for each hand before reaching up for higher ones. But it was not always possible to do this without attempting hazardous reaches toward ledges of rock and bits of vegetation too far away to be tested first for strength and reliability. Sometimes a man had to manage with one handhold and one foot support, or with two foot supports while sliding the palms of the hands up against the rock face in search of higher holds. Others were forced to relieve one hand by slipping the other hand, finger by finger, into the same crevice, and searching sideways for additional support with whatever leg happened at the moment to be hanging free. They used their knees as well as their hands and feet in their endless exploration for outcrops of rock and vegetation, and more than once they had to stop and wait until a leg suffering from muscle fatigue stopped shaking.

At one point, about 150 feet up the rock face, Kasper Idland could get only one handhold, and from it he dangled, concentrating all his strength and determination in his fingers while feeling with his free hand along the rock for chinks and crevices. There was nothing to the left of him except inch-deep cracks full of rock dust that the thaw had made wet and slippery. He switched hands on the one hold he did have and tried the other side, reaching up and down and back and forth in overlapping fashion until he found the beginning of a tangle of growth to his right. By swinging his body back and forth, he was just able to touch the tangle of growth with his outstretched fingers. But he could not get a grip on it, and he did not want to let go until he did. He had to do something, though, before the last of the strength in his fingers gave out.

Trying desperately to separate the sound of panic in his breathing from that caused by his efforts, he made one final swing, letting go with his left hand and grabbing with his right at the same time. For a split second, he had no hold at all. Luckily, the tangle of growth extended downward as well as to the right; it took his full weight like something consciously alive. Gasping for breath, his eyes burning from sweat, he dug through the pine needles to the bark as a sudden gust of wind ripped along the rock face with such persistence that even as it raced past him, it seemed fastened upon him.

A minute sooner, he thought, if this wind had hit like this a minute sooner, I'd be down at the bottom of the gorge now.

Every move by every man carried with it the possibility of a fall into the gorge below, where the huge slabs of ice on the river would be as hard and sharp against bone and flesh as the rocks along the shore. This knowledge—that it would be futile in the event of a fall to kick out from the rock face and try to land in the river—added to the tension as the men heaved and strained and tried with sticky tongues to wet their crusted lips. At the same time, the tension added to the danger, for it had the unexpected effect of increasing each man's desire to keep up with the others. If two or three fell behind, they struggled that much harder to catch up, and when they did, the others were spurred to new efforts not to fall behind themselves. This further increased the pace as they clambered higher and higher toward their goal—the shelf of rock along which the railway tracks ran.

From their training in Britain, they all knew that they were not to look down or back, but as they approached their exhaustion level and their toes and fingers stiffened, as their Tommy guns and ammunition and packs of explosives grew heavier and more burdensome, the temptation to look down became harder and harder to resist. Two or three, grim-faced, panting, and determined to go on, but continually shaken in their resolve not to look down, finally did so. The gorge below, wedged in by the walls of rock on either side, appeared extremely narrow, with the river forming a winding string of silver through its middle. The sight of it was like a trap, holding them immobile where they were, between the distance they had climbed and the distance they had still to climb. The movement of a single muscle suddenly seemed full of risk and peril, so entranced were they by the sight below, their own rigidity, and the racing of their minds and imaginations. Only the sound and sight of their struggling comrades restored their grit and resolution as they turned upward again, their bodies straining against the stone, to reach for higher holds.

During such a mission nothing is more remarkable than the power of those involved to ward off the full impact of what is happening until after their struggles have brought them through it. Even after all nine men had safely reached the shelf of rock on which the railway ran, there persisted throughout their gasping struggle for breath an inclination to doubt the reality of the feat they had just accomplished. Rönneberg said nothing for several minutes, and neither did anyone else. They had reached the tracks without being detected, and for the time being that was enough. A languidness overcame them, so soothing that for a moment they thought they might get the better of the German guards just by smiling at them. It was only a few minutes past eleven anyway, and the two main buildings, their grayish-white forms like huge outcrops of rock in the mountainside itself, were less than half a mile away.

Gradually, as their breathing subsided and their hearts

stopped pounding, they became aware once more of the plant's hum. Carried by a downward-flowing westerly wind, the sound of turbines and machinery reached their ears with the rhythmic cadence of normal industrial activity. Every worker was doing his routine job; the German guards were doing theirs. The idea was both reassuring and sobering to the nine men, who knew that everything depended upon their not upsetting the plant's routine.

"All right, men," Rönneberg said, restrapping his rucksack of explosives to his back, "let's get closer. The covering party will lead the way."

Knut Haukelid, the leader of the covering party, immediately started forward along the tracks, followed Indian file by Kjelstrup, Helberg, Storhaug, and Poulsson. Good luck, Rönneberg thought, for it was clearly understood that if the Germans had indeed placed land mines around the tracks, and anyone in the covering party stepped on one, every man not killed or wounded by shrapnel would fight his way into the plant if necessary to get the job done.

Rönneberg and the demolition men, who were carrying enough explosives to blow a gaping hole in the side of the mountain, waited until about fifty yards separated them from Poulsson, the last man in the covering party. Then they started forward, always remaining about the same distance behind and always stepping in the path made by the men in the covering party. Meanwhile, Haukelid, far out in front of everybody, had luckily found a trodden path in the snow beside the railway ties. On the assumption that only authorized persons could have made the path, he carefully followed it and was thus followed by the others. Coming to a snow-covered shed housing a small transformer station about 500 yards from the plant, he turned around and received a relayed signal from Rönneberg to halt.

When the men reassembled at the shed, the steady throbbing of the plant sounded much louder, and seemed somehow to add to the dimensions of the task facing them.

"We have a good view from here," Rönneberg said, "so we'll

wait until the two German guards on the bridge are relieved." He glanced at his watch. "That'll be at midnight, half an hour from now."

A few of the men stepped into the transformer shed to avoid the wind, which kept cooling their snow-wet uniforms and the sweat that had moistened their underclothing during their grueling climb to the railway tracks. Others got behind the shed, and looked up at the sky streaked with clouds and moonlight, or across the valley toward the cable-car lift, where the Ryes Road, their planned route of escape, zigzagged its way up to Hardanger Plateau. Since the wind and the noise from the plant precluded the need for silence, they gradually became engaged in what Rønneberg later recalled as the most pedestrian conversations with one another. Nibbling on the food they had stuffed in their pockets, pointing out lights here and there across the valley, where houses clung to the mountainside at Våer, they might have been plant workers enjoying a coffee break.

Rønneberg looked in wonder at Kjelstrup picking his teeth with the splintered end of a match, and listened with delight to Helberg telling someone about the ant-covered syrup he had found in the hut in Fjøsbudalen. The more prosaically they acted, the more unreasonably he admired them. Their voices in the dark belong emphatically to them, he thought, and at the same time to the night of which they are a part. He had never felt so close to them before, or less limited in his imagination by what they were saying. There was a sense of being both with them and somewhere else, a stranger and a friend, part of the mission and part of something happening back in Britain. Just looking at the snow-covered shed where the men had congregated was like being inside it, listening to Helberg talk was like being Helberg. He could see their mothers in their voices, the holiday dinners they had sat down to at home, their boyhood fishing trips beside fjords where their hopes and still-unformulated personal ambitions had first taken root. They might have left everything but their souls behind in the hut in Fjösbudalen, there was that little to impede the sense that they were seeing the world from the same broad balcony.

"With the attack drawing near, I expected great tension among the men, or unnatural attempts at humor," Rönneberg recalled. "But no. It was amazing how they acted. If there had been a camera trained on us, the scene it recorded would have been a relaxed one—a group of men eating, watching the lights from Våer, across the valley, and chatting. Just a group of friends talking. Those minutes gave everyone great confidence."

At exactly three minutes before midnight, they all watched in silence as two German soldiers left the barracks in the plant's yard and started down the hill toward the suspension bridge to relieve the two guards on duty there. A few minutes later, the two relieved guards started up the hill toward the barracks. Though each carried a rifle, their trudging steps expressed a weariness born of repetition and routine. One was taller than the other, and he was doing the talking. He seemed to be trying to convince the other of something, and although he never stopped walking, he had a way of throwing his chest out and up like someone sitting behind a desk. His heedlessness of danger fascinated Rönneberg and his men, for it heightened their shared knowledge of what was about to happen. It was almost as if they were imagining what they were seeing, or remembering something they had seen in the past. If the mission succeeded and they all escaped without injury, this moment would be one of the ones they would all remember.

"We'll have to wait," Rönneberg said after the two German soldiers had entered the barracks and closed the door behind them. "Another half hour, to give the men relieving them time to relax."

As the minutes passed, they fell more and more under the spell of the plant's tempo of production, which had the same effect on them that a tom-tom has on Indians preparing for battle. The more dully the sound repeated itself, the more agitated they became. Rönneberg, one of those men who both thrive on the tension of others and are made calmer by it, checked once more to make sure that every man was certain about his part in the operation and understood his orders. Going from one man to another, he quietly gave them facts and contingencies to put between themselves and their emotions.

At exactly 12:30, they advanced along the tracks to some store sheds about 100 yards from the gate.

"Arne," Rönneberg said to Kjelstrup, "go to the gate and cut the chain. The rest of the covering party will go with you and fan out in support. Once the gate is open, signal. We'll stand by to follow up immediately."

After numerous delays, near-starvation, incredible hardship, and one of the worst winters in the history of Hardanger Plateau, the mission to prevent Nazi Germany from developing an atomic bomb was at last about to start its final phase. Roosevelt and Churchill were not watching, but in Washington and London they were waiting. They knew what Rönneberg and his men only sensed: that the very course of history depended upon whether or not the mission succeeded.

13

Everyone's tension and anxiety found an object in the familiar slope of the former plumber's shoulders as he tightened the bite of the armorer's shears against a link in the padlocked chain. For Kjelstrup himself, the simple application of leverage was like performing a familiar plumbing chore back in Oslo. It relieved him to exert pressure to make the three-quarter-inch steel open wider, its clean insides showing, like a cut finger before the blood begins to flow. Then the chain parted and fell loose against the gate with a jangle that only he could hear. At his touch the gate swung open, and that was all the signal the covering party needed. Within seconds Haukelid and the others were through the gate with him, fanning out to take up temporary positions according to plan.

The electrolysis building had appeared large and formidable from the other side of the valley. Now, from less than fifty yards away, it appeared as mammoth as the mountainside on which it stood. Its mere presence made the danger real. Like nothing else, it placed them inside the plant's grounds, where even their familiarity with one another came as a surprise.

The demolition party, led by Rönneberg, had meanwhile opened a second gate a short distance from the railway gate with another pair of shears. This would provide them with an alternative escape route in the event they were pursued after the explosion.

"I stopped and listened," Rönneberg remembered. "So far we had not been detected. The hum of the machinery was steady and normal. There was a good light from the moon, with no one in sight except our own men."

At a given signal from him, everyone in the covering party advanced to his assigned position. Kjelstrup turned left at the electrolysis building to keep an eye on the German sentry patrolling the penstocks running some 900 feet above the plant. Helberg set himself up near the two open gates to cover the retreat after the explosion. Storhaug, "The Chicken," his pistol in its holster, his Tommy gun in his hand, hurried forward to where the road led down from the yard to the suspension bridge, to see that the guards on the bridge did not come up toward the factory area.

Haukelid and Poulsson started through the yard toward the German barracks. Bending slightly forward at the waist, like athletes at the ready, Haukelid armed with tubes of chloroform to overcome any Norwegian watchman they might encounter, Poulsson with his finger on the trigger of his Tommy gun, they edged their way along the rear of the office building. From there they hurried across to the wall of the power plant, then out into the open yard to where two storage tanks stood directly opposite the barracks. With their boots scraping against the yard's gritty pavement, they scrambled from one tank to another to see if they could give themselves a better view of the entire yard, or a wider angle from which to shoot, in the event the twelve soldiers in the barracks attempted to run out at the sound of an alarm. High above them, where the black-painted windows of the electrolysis building had been scratched or slightly broken, bits of light scattered downward through the darkness, dotting the space between them and the barracks with what seemed a thousand eyes.

"Good spot," Poulsson said, nodding toward the barracks door. "Only a few feet away."

The demolition party, which had advanced almost simultaneously with the covering party, had reached the electrolysis building. Rönneberg, Kayser, Strömsheim, and Idland converged on the steel door leading to the basement in anticipation of getting in before a guard or watchman came along.

"Locked!" Rönneberg whispered.

Though he had more than enough explosive to blow the door open, he remembered what he had been told in Britain by Tronstad, on the basis of his briefing about the plant's layout by Brun. "If you try to force the door to the basement," he had said, "you will probably raise an alarm that will result in a struggle with the German soldiers and many casualties. The killing of German soldiers will result in heavy reprisals by the German military against Norwegian civilians. I therefore advise you to use the cable duct for entrance into the plant."

"Try the door up on the ground floor," Rönneberg told Strömsheim and Idland.

Just seeing them run up the concrete stairs in their British uniforms was like being reminded that their luck could not last much longer. Here they were, in the plant's yard, as close to the German barracks as they were to their objective, and not a single guard or watchman had appeared. The idea astonished him even as it prodded him on to speedier action. Racing to his right around the northwest corner of the building, with Kayser close behind, he came to a ground-level window. Like all the other windows in the building, it had been blacked out with paint, but where the vertical and horizontal sashes intersected, there were clear, keyhole-sized specks of glass that the paintbrush had missed.

As Rönneberg hunched forward to look through one of these, Kayser, guarding him from behind with a Colt .45, could see the working of his shoulder muscles, the torqued neck bunched with knots and cartilage. Everything about him expressed imperativeness rather than fear.

Suddenly, with a smile that came and went like lightning, he turned round to Kayser, pointed toward the window, and nodded. Six feet below the window was their target, the high-concentration room itself, with its two parallel sets of heavy-water cells. Sitting in the middle of the room, at a table set up between the two rows of cells, was a Norwegian workman writing something in a book.

They could break the window and enter this way. Why not? Only glass separated them from the heavy-water apparatus they had come to destroy, and every second counted. But the sound of the breaking glass might frighten the man. He might start running and shouting, and if he did, they would have to kill him, an innocent Norwegian.

"The cable tunnel," Rönneberg said, and continued to his right in search of it, alongside the snow piled high against the building by the plant's plow. Just beyond the northeast corner of the building, he saw a ladder two or three rungs deep in snow, leading up to what looked like a hole, or the mouth of a small cave, in the rock and concrete beside the building's east wall.

"Here it is," he called to Kayser, and started up the ladder. There was no time to waste. Strömsheim and Idland would find the cable tunnel themselves. If they didn't, he had all the necessary explosives in his rucksack to do the job himself.

Going in headfirst, with Kayser behind him, he encountered a maze of pipes and cables separated by just enough space to accommodate a prone man's body.

"The space was so narrow I could not look back," Rönneberg said later, "but I knew Kayser was behind me. I could hear him breathing."

"My job was to cover Rönneberg while he placed the charges around the high-concentration cells," Kayser said, "so I stayed with him all the way."

Using a small flashlight, Rönneberg kept his eyes on three things, the cables and pipes in front of him and the concrete flooring over which he was crawling. If there was a bendable cable in the way, or a loose replacement for some pipe fitting on the concrete flooring, he carefully moved it. His breathing came short and gaspy, but that was from the care and concentration of his crawl, the tension in every cell and fiber of his body. The danger the mission posed to his own life, the consideration that, if fighting broke out between the Germans and the covering party, he would almost certainly die in this building, did not detain him. Being a living, loyal Norwegian meant doing this. His universe was the immediate task before him, these thirty-odd yards of tunnel.

At about the halfway point, he came to some water pipelines passing into the high-concentration room through a hole in the tunnel's concrete flooring. Between these pipes and the concrete there was just enough space for him to see the Norwegian workman, who was still making notations in his book at the table. Relieved that the man was alone and occupied, he was just about to start forward again when Kayser, squeezing through a tight space behind him, leaned forward too far. His Colt slipped out of his shoulder holster and fell on one of the pipes. Poisoned with despair and terror, the blood deserting their legs in its mad rush heartward, they waited, expecting at any moment to hear an alarm sounded.

"There was a clear metallic sound," Kayser said later, "the kind of sound that carries far and draws attention."

In the silence that followed, their breathing was like a sharing of emotions. For weeks in Scotland they had practiced placing charges on dummy high-concentration cells. Now, with the actual cells only yards away, was this one mishap about to ruin their chances?

Rönneberg peered between the pipes again. No, the man was at his table, still making notations. Apparently the building was full of odd noises.

Inching themselves the rest of the way, past webs of piping that made them wince and utter prayerlike curses, they finally came to an open hole in the tunnel about ten feet above the basement floor. About the size of a manhole, it led to a basement room adjacent to the target.

"Every minute was now valuable," Rönneberg wrote in his report. "As there was no sign of Strömsheim and Idland, Kayser and I decided to carry on the demolition alone."

Lowering themselves through the hole to the basement floor, they drew their guns and started toward the high-concentration room.

NO ADMITTANCE EXCEPT ON BUSINESS. The notice on the

door, which was, surprisingly, fitted with only a Yale lock, brought a grin to Rönneberg's face as he turned the knob and swung the door wide open. The Norwegian workman, sitting with his back to them at the table, was taken completely by surprise. In fact, he had to remove his glasses to bring the two intruders into focus.

"On your feet. Hands up!" Kayser said. "Where's the key to the steel door leading to the yard?"

This was the door they had found locked earlier, the door through which they planned to escape after the explosion. When the man handed him the key, Kayser led him at gunpoint over against a wall.

"Nothing will happen to you if you do as you are told. We're British soldiers."

He pointed to the British insignia on his uniform so the man would have no doubt about what to tell the Germans afterward. If the man simply told the truth—that British soldiers in uniform had sabotaged the plant—there would be no reprisals against innocent Norwegians in the area.

"What's your name?" Kayser went on.

"Gustav Johansen."

"Keep talking to him about Britain," Rönneberg told Kayser in English.

He quickly locked the door to the room, "so we could work in peace," dragged the man's table over to a corner, opened his rucksack, and laid out his twenty-odd explosive charges. Already he was immersed in this situation and no other, doing precisely what he had imagined for weeks he would be doing. Each charge was sausage-shaped, about twelves inches long, and composed of nitrocellulose, an adhesive, puttylike, plastic explosive. There was a detonator fuse, 120 centimeters long, extending from each one, and since it took one second for each centimeter of fuse to burn, the full-length fuse had a burning time of 120 seconds.

Slipping on rubber gloves as a precaution against electric shock while touching the high-concentration cells, Rönneberg took the first charge and went to work. The eighteen cells looked extremely intricate and complicated, with lead pipes, condenser tubes, sand seals, water seals, rubber connections, anodes, cathodes, asbestos diaphragms, water jackets, and flanges, but he did not have to stop and think about what he was doing, for they were the exact duplicates of those he had practiced on in Britain. All eighteen were identical: four feet, two inches high, twelve inches in diameter, and jacketed in heavy-gauge stainless steel.

"Our explosives fit around the apparatus like a glove," Rönneberg recalled. "You just pressed them around and against the cylindrical metal containers, and they stuck."

Johansen, his hands held high above his head, kept watching Rönneberg with both fear and surprise. These were the only high-concentration heavy-water cells in all of Europe, and Rönneberg went from one to another, wrapping a charge just below the water jacket of each one, where the cell was most vulnerable, as though he had been sabotaging nothing but high-concentration cells all his life. Certainly it was not a technique he could have thought of on the spur of the moment.

"I think you should know that there is a lye leakage," Johansen said, as if to establish his own familiarity with the cells. "It is very caustic, so be careful not to get any on your skin or clothing."

Rönneberg had been told in Britain that the night man in the high-concentration room was a "good Norwegian," an anti-Nazi who would give them no trouble.

"Thank you," Rönneberg said, and went on with the job. He was just about to wrap a charge around the ninth cell when a sudden crash of glass broke the silence. Kayser swung his gun from Johansen to a window opening on the back yard. His finger had just started to squeeze the trigger when he saw Strömsheim's face framed in jagged glass.

"I almost killed him," Kayser said later. "If there had been a bullet in the chamber of my gun, I probably would have. I recognized him just in time."

Strömsheim and Idland, unable to find the cable duct, had decided to act on their own initiative. Rönneberg rushed to the window ("enough time had been lost already") and began dislodging the jagged pieces of glass from around the frame so Strömsheim could climb down into the room and help him place the charges. In his haste, he cut his hand badly despite the rubber gloves he was wearing.

"Stay outside and cover this broken window," he told Idland, after Strömsheim had lowered himself into the room with another rucksack of explosives.

Quickly wrapping a handkerchief around his bleeding hand, Rönneberg began coupling the fuses while Strömsheim placed the remaining charges. There were eighteen fuses altogether, and the idea was to couple them so that there would be just nine to ignite. Eight would be 120 centimeters long, and the ninth would be cut to thirty centimeters. Rönneberg would ignite the longer, two-minute fuses first, then, just before they made a run for it, the shortened fuse. This last, thirty-second, fuse would detonate all eighteen charges simultaneously; the two-minute fuses would serve as insurance against anything happening to the shortened fuse. This arrangement had been set up in London by Colonel Wilson and Leif Tronstad, who did not want to run the risk of someone getting to the charges and defusing them before they exploded.

When Strömsheim had placed the last charge, he checked all eighteen of them, twice, to make sure they were all securely wrapped around the cells. Then he and Rönneberg checked the entire arrangement, fuses and charges, once more, before ignition.

"All right," Rönneberg said to Kayser, "let's get that door to the yard unlocked."

Kayser quickly led Johansen at gunpoint from the high-concentration room into the outer basement room, where the heavy steel door leading to the yard was encased in reinforced concrete a foot and a half thick. This was the door that the Germans had said should be locked at all times, and when Kayser handed the key to Johansen, he told him, "Unlock it quietly. Make sure you don't make any noise."

After Johansen carefully turned the key in the lock, Kayser swung the door an eighth of an inch on its hinges to make sure the bolt had been withdrawn.

"It's not that I don't trust you," he said. "I'm just not allowed to trust anybody."

"I understand," Johansen said.

The moment they returned to the high-concentration room, Rönneberg, who during their absence had scattered several British parachute badges around the room as "visiting cards," struck a match and, with blood dripping like sweat from his fingers, started toward the longer fuses. There was no sign of alarm from the yard, and this added to their desire to ignite the fuses and escape while luck was still with them.

"Wait, please," Johansen said. "My eyeglasses. They're on the table. I need them for my job. They're almost impossible to replace these days."

The extremity of the moment seemed to add to Rönneberg's self-control. From intelligence reports he knew that there were armed German guards on other floors inside the building. Any one of them might drop by unexpectedly. But he also knew that the Nazis had seized all of Norway's optical goods and equipment. He blew out the match, went to the desk in the far corner of the room, and found the man's glasses case.

"Here," he said.

"*Tusan takk,*" Johansen said, using the familiar Norwegian "Thousand thanks."

Rönneberg went back to the fuses with another lighted match. Bending over, he was about to light the first one when Johansen said in an anguished voice, "I beg you, wait! My glasses! They are not in the case."

He spoke as if some principle touching upon the rules of war were involved. He had done nothing to impede their sabotage efforts; why should they prevent him from retrieving his glasses?

Rönneberg, the muscles in his jaw working, swung back toward the obviously sincere man and blew out the second match. The whole thing was like the absurdity at the heart of war. Roosevelt and Churchill, not to mention every British, American, and Norwegian scientist connected with atomic research, were awaiting the result of this top-priority sabotage mission. If it failed, the war against Hitler might be lost, but because the same war had made eyeglasses irreplaceable, the fate of the mission hung in doubt. If a German guard from one of the upper floors suddenly appeared, Kayser might have to shoot him. Before dying, the German guard might get off a shot or two. The shots would undoubtedly alert other German guards. If they arrived in time to cut off the burning fuses, the Germans would have their heavy-water apparatus intact.

"Where *are* your damn glasses?" Rönneberg whispered in a frenzy to the man.

He rushed back to the desk, rummaged through the papers and books, and finally found the glasses between the leaves of the logbook in which Johansen had been making notations earlier.

"Here, *take* them!" Rönneberg said.

"*Tusan takk,*" Johansen said again.

Rönneberg had no sooner struck the third match than what he dreaded most happened. Strömsheim, guarding the doorway through which they planned to escape, heard footsteps on the stairs. A German guard from one of the upper floors was on his way down. The pressure now was on Rönneberg. In the seconds remaining before the guard appeared, should he light the fuses in order to save time, or wait until they held up or killed the guard? The tension in the room seemed to pass into him and become something else, something that added to his courage and determination.

Kayser had Johansen covered; Strömsheim had his pistol out and ready, and after a second's hesitation Rönneberg blew out the third match and grabbed his own gun. The suspense was almost palpable; it webbed the air and made it hard to breathe.

Quietly and innocently, a Norwegian civilian appeared. It was Gunnar Engebretsen, the night foreman, coming down on his inspection tour. Seeing Johansen with his hands up and the three men in British army uniforms, he blinked several times, a scribble of disbelief in his eyes, as though his sanity depended upon his being able to fathom the presence of British soldiers inside Vemork's high-concentration room, the most important room to the Nazis in all of Norway. There were German guards all around the plant. The suspension bridge was guarded, the penstocks mined. And he had heard no shots. How did you get here? His eyes cried out as he raised his hands high.

"Get them both over next to the stairs," Rönneberg told Kayser. "After I light the short fuse, tell them to start running up the stairs as fast as they can. They should reach the second floor before the explosion."

"What could be holding them up?" Poulsson said. Haukelid shook his head. "I wish I knew."

They had been waiting behind the storage tanks opposite the barracks for twenty-five minutes, but it seemed like hours. Nothing at all had happened; no German guard or Norwegian watchman had appeared, no sound other than the whirring of the dynamos had reached their ears. The monotony of the tension only made it worse, for it kept building on the same speculative note: Has the demolition party been trapped inside the building?

For Helberg, Kjelstrup, and Storhaug, each alone at his post, the anxiety of waiting was worse for being solitary. Storhaug especially counted time by the throbbing of his heart. Standing amongst some fir trees near a turn in the road leading down to the bridge, he could plainly see, through a narrow lane between the pine needles, the two German guards on duty there. They were talking in voices free of the slightest suspicion that anyone was listening, and this deepened the uncomfortable intimacy he felt in being this close to them in a British uniform. He might at any moment have to kill them, and in the meantime he had to listen to them say commonplace things that made anything as momentous as killing them seem brutally inappropriate. But this was where he had to stay until he heard the explosion. Like an unwilling confidant to the two Germans, he waited.

Meanwhile, in the basement of the electrolysis building, the time for the explosion was drawing near, the long, two-minute, fuses were burning away, and Rönneberg was about to ignite the short one. Strömsheim had strapped his rucksack full of unused explosives to his back, and Kayser had escorted Engebretsen and Johansen at gunpoint to the concrete stairs.

"You should make it up two floors before the explosion," he told the two Norwegians. "But don't start until I tell you."

The fascination of watching the fuses burn blinded him to the danger the explosion posed to his own life. He remembered what Tronstad had told them on their departure from Britain: "You have a fifty-fifty chance of doing the job, and only a fair chance of escaping."

Now, as Rönneberg ignited the shortened fuse and said "Go!" Kayser became more determined than ever that they would at least do the job.

"I counted to ten before I let the two Norwegians go," he said later, "so there would be absolutely no possibility of the fuses being choked off before the explosion. Then I told them, 'Run! Run as fast as you can!' "

He caught up with Rönneberg and Strömsheim at the steel door leading to the yard. They opened it, closed it behind them, and found Idland, Tommy gun in hand, outside waiting for them. Rönneberg took time to shake hands with him before they started running. They were only twenty yards from the cellar door when they heard the explosion. Muffled by the building's thick concrete walls, it sounded more like a thud, but, glancing back, they could see the flash of flame reflected on the snow outside the basement's blown-out windows, and feel the whoosh of air against their legs.

"We passed through the gate and climbed up to the railway tracks," Rönneberg wrote in his report. "For a moment I looked back down the line and listened. Except for the faint hum of the machinery, the same hum we had heard when we arrived, everything in the factory was quiet."

To Poulsson and Haukelid, the explosion sounded astonishingly feeble and insignificant. Still guarding the barracks from their post behind the storage tanks, they glanced with dismay at each other. Was this what they had spent months of training in Britain, weeks of freezing up in the mountains, and hours of climbing a precipitous gorge to accomplish? They heard the splintering crash of the basement windows being blown out, and saw the orange flash cut like lightning through the darkness, but somehow, perhaps because their pent-up emotions demanded more, they expected more.

Nor did the Germans respond with alarm, let alone in force. Several seconds passed before the barracks door was flung open and a single German soldier, bareheaded and unarmed, appeared, silhouetted in the light behind him. Glancing up toward the tiers of open balconies running along the walls of the electrolysis building, he shook his head, walked over to the steel door leading into the plant, found it locked, as usual, and returned to the barracks.

The muffled sound of the explosion notwithstanding, Poulsson and Haukelid could not understand his apparent lack of concern. What they did not know was that similar "explosions" occasionally occurred up on the building's balconies, in burners used for regaining deuterium from hydrogen gas by combustion. The workers at the plant called these burners "cannons," because of their appearance, the noise they made, and the way they kept the German guards on edge.

"The burners were situated in free air on the balconies of the hydrogen factory building," Jomar Brun has explained. "Small explosions, rather heavy bangs, occurred occasionally—every day, every second day, or once a week, depending on circumstances.

"For example, if a burner had been turned off and was to be put into operation again, it sometimes happened that the ignition started with a bang. Explosions with heavy bangs also happened occasionally when the flow of gas (hydrogen and oxygen) to a burner for some reason became sluggish."

The German soldier had obviously heard many such explosions. This explains why he looked up toward the building's balconies, and also why the guards on the bridge did not come running up to investigate. The muffled sound of the explosion, snatched away by the wind, had reached their ears as so many cannon explosions had in the past.

Poulsson and Haukelid were just about to leave their post and escape with the others along the railway tracks when the barracks door was flung open again, by the same German soldier.

"He's back!" Poulsson whispered. "He must suspect something."

Armed this time with a rifle and searchlight, the soldier started over toward where they were hiding. He held the rifle in his left hand with the relaxed attitude of a workman carrying a tool, while playing the beam of light to the left and right along the ground in front of him. Poulsson, tensing his trigger finger to see if the muscles would work, waited imploringly for him to shrug and go back in again. He did not want innocent people, let alone his own mother, father, brother, and two sisters to suffer if he had to kill, but the soldier kept coming closer and closer.

"Shall I fire?"

"Not yet. Wait'll he sees us."

Poulsson thought of their training in Britain, how they had been taught to shoot only one bullet at a time from a Tommy gun. If he had to kill the man, he would try to do it with just one bullet, making as little noise as possible. That way, they might be able to escape without killing others as well. The more Germans they killed, the more severe the reprisals would be.

For no apparent reason, the soldier suddenly cast the beam of light into the air, then swung it back down again, this time on the ground behind where Poulsson and Haukelid were hiding. If he now swung it to the foreground again, to cover the stretch of darkness he had missed, his life would be over. He hesitated, as if puzzling over something, then, in answer to what seemed another causeless change of mind, glanced once more up toward the balconies of the electrolysis building and returned to the barracks.

"We assumed he thought the tumbling mountain snow from the thaw had exploded one of the land mines placed alongside the penstocks," Poulsson said later.

Neither he nor Haukelid (nor anyone else connected with the mission) knew about the occasional explosions in the cannons on the balconies. It was the one gap in their intelligence about the plant, but it made no difference now, for the mission had been accomplished and they were on their way, racing through the yard toward the railway gate.

As they approached it, they heard the hoarsely whispered word "Piccadilly?"

"It was so obviously the voice of Arne Kjelstrup," Poulsson recalled, "that we didn't even bother to give the password, 'Leicester Square!'"

But Kjelstrup, on edge from his lonely wait at the rear of the electrolysis building, would not be put off. "Piccadilly?" he whispered again.

"By this time we had lost patience," Poulsson said. "I told him, 'For God's sake, shut up.'"

"Why have passwords if we're not going to use them?" Kjelstrup shot back.

Helberg, meanwhile, had gone ahead along the tracks to make sure everyone in the demolition party had escaped.

"They're all up ahead on the tracks," he said, rushing back.

"What about Storhaug?" Haukelid said.

"He's with them."

Haukelid swung the railway gate shut behind them and carefully draped the chain and padlock into position. No sense in letting the Germans know how and where the plant had been entered.

"All right, let's go!"

As they hurried along the trodden path by the tracks to catch up, Poulsson shouted to Haukelid, "You better get rid of that chloroform. Before you mash a tube and chloroform yourself."

"I already have," Haukelid said.

Not only had he got rid of it, but he had also carefully removed his fingerprints before throwing the box away. The Germans had taken his fingerprints when he was arrested in 1941, and he, too, had relatives in Norway, relatives who would be tortured if his fingerprints were traced.

"Besides," Poulsson shouted as they ran, "don't you know the use of gas is forbidden in this war?"

Rönneberg and the others in the demolition party were waiting for them about 300 yards from the railway gate. Poulsson expected changes in their appearance, subtle disclosures of what placing the charges had done to them. Except for the blood-stained wrapping around Rönneberg's hand, though, they looked too familiar to reveal anything he didn't already know about them. When Poulsson asked about the bloody hand, Rönneberg shrugged. "Nothing. Just a cut."

"The Germans still don't seem to know what's happened," Haukelid said.

They had expected and been prepared for a desperate struggle, the loss of at least one or two men, but so far nothing like that had happened. The mission was accomplished, not a single shot had been fired, and they were all still together and still alive. The idea was like a powerful drunkenness filled with visions of escape. Even Kasper Idland, who had put no faith in the possibility of escape, began to change his mind.

"Let's get going," he said.

But an enemy far more powerful than the German soldiers now faced them—the treacherous foehn, which had doubled in power in the last hour. The men could feel the warm air against their faces and see the snow turning to mush around their boots. They would be up to their waists in it on the way back up to Hardanger Plateau—if they ever reached the other side of the valley.

"Helberg will lead the way," Rönneberg said.

Remembering their dangerous climb up to the railway tracks, Helberg hurried along until he came to what looked like a less precipitous descent into the gorge below. The rock face here supported no vegetation and was covered with melting, slushy snow, but if they made good use of the twists and turns in the rock face, and stopped at ledges to slow their descent, they should have no trouble.

He led the way, and they all followed, with an alacrity bordering on greed. Sliding, stopping, and then sliding again, they all safely reached the bottom of the gorge, where the broken and parted floor of ice on the river looked like the result of an earth tremor. Huge slabs of it were jammed together, piled on top of one another, or thrown by the swollen river against the bank on either side. The water kept sluicing between them, around and over them, creating foaming peaks and coiling eddies as white as the ice itself.

As they started across, each man stepping on slabs of ice of his own choosing, the cross-reverberations in the gorge itself were suddenly drowned out by sirens signaling a general mobilization of troops and collaborationist police in the Rjukan area.

"When the sirens were turned on," Poulsson remembers, "it was as if we were being pursued across the river by the shrieking sound itself. We slipped and fell, grabbing on to rocks and blocks of ice, it didn't matter which."

Once on the other side, they started climbing. There was no need to speak or for Rönneberg to urge them to hurry. If the floodlights on the roof of the plant were turned on and they were seen, they would be trapped where they were, in the gorge, with German troops above and on each side of them. They had to get out immediately, and they all knew it.

At the plant, the stair wells, floors, and balconies were being searched by German soldiers convinced that the saboteurs were still on the premises. They knew that no one had attempted to cross the suspension bridge or to come down the mountainside alongside the penstocks leading to the plant. Since the gorge itself was looked upon as impassable, the saboteurs must be either in the plant or hiding somewhere around it.

The only two men who had actually seen the saboteurs, Engebretsen and Johansen, had followed Kayser's orders and raced up the concrete stairs to avoid the explosion. Having been held up an extra ten seconds before being released, they had hardly reached the second landing when they heard and felt the tremendous destructive power of the charges going off. In point of fact, there was nothing "feeble and insignificant" about the explosion inside the building. No German guard or Norwegian workman on any of the floors confused the sound with the occasional "bangs" of the cannons on the balconies around the building. Indeed, Johansen and Engebretsen, continuing on up the stairs to report to the Norwegian engineer on duty, had just reached the first floor of the building, one floor above the ground floor, when they were met by a German guard and a Norwegian watchman rushing down the stairs to investigate.

"I was on the third floor of the building when the charges went off," said Ivar Nass, one of the plant's engineers, later. "The explosion was tremendous; the power of it reverberated throughout the entire building. But outside, it may not have sounded like much, maybe like one of the 'cannons' on the balcony. The building's concrete walls are very thick."

Chief Engineer Alf H. Larsen, who had succeeded Jomar Brun as head of the plant, was a guest at a bridge party at a neighbor's house just outside Vemork's main gate, on the plant side of the gorge, when he heard the explosion. Telephoning the plant to find out what had happened, he was told by Engebretsen, edgy from being held at gunpoint in the high-concentration room, that the heavy-water plant had been blown up. Larsen immediately telephoned the news to Bjårne Nilssen, director of Norsk Hydro in the Rjukan-Vemork area, who said he would be there directly. Before rushing out to his wood-burning motorcar, Nilssen called another number and alerted the German garrison at Rjukan.

Larsen left the bridge party and rushed up to the plant's high-concentration room to assess the damage.

"When I got in, through the door," he said later, "I could see that all the high-concentration cells had been blown up. The bottom was knocked out of each individual cell. I could also see that the whole room was full of sprays of water, this obviously having been caused by shrapnel from the explosion having penetrated the water tubes of the plant's cooling system. Being in the room was actually, well, like being in a shower. And it then struck me that this was a perfect sabotage."

Meanwhile, Rönneberg and his men, unable to understand why the floodlights atop the plant had not been turned on along with the sirens, were clambering up the other side of the gorge toward the very highway the troops would be using on their way from Rjukan to the plant. They knew there would be no lorry or supporting force waiting to rescue them, and this knowledge in the darkness, coupled with the still-startling realization that not a single shot had been fired, intensified their desire to get away.

"During our retreat, the psychological and nervous pressure increased tremendously," Rönneberg said later. "It was not that we had overprepared ourselves for the mission. We just wanted more than ever, now that the mission was accomplished, to save our lives as well."

They were living sheerly on nerves now, but this did not hamper them or make them tremble or slip or make mistakes in climbing. On the contrary, it increased their awareness of every rock, branch, and bush they touched, made them more responsive to changes in the power of the wind, to nuances in the cloud-streaked moonlight. Climbing hand over hand, fighting for holds for their feet, and yet always careful not to start a snowslide that would take them back down into the gorge again, they finally reached the highway. As they were about to cross it, a car came around a bend on its way to Vemork. Just watching it approach was like remembering to be frightened. They waited, quieter than they really had to be, as the headlights swung toward them in response to a turn in the road. It was Nilssen, driving to the plant in his wood-burning automobile. They had no idea who he was, and he appeared too engrossed in negotiating the precipitous curves to notice anything or anyone on either side of him.

After he passed, they splashed their way across the highway through water streaming like a river between melting banks of snow, then struggled up through the brush to where they had hidden their skis and rucksacks on the power-line road. Already they could see the beams of headlights from trucks carrying German troops from Rjukan, and the beams of flashlights directly opposite them on the other side of the gorge, where soldiers, following the trail of blood from Rönneberg's hand, were raking the railway ties with light along their line of retreat. The hunt was on, and they were still in the valley, soaking wet, in British uniforms that they were forbidden to remove.

"We had a hard time making our way through the woods above the highway until we reached the power-line road," Poulsson recalled. "There we felt as exposed as pins on a bowling alley. There was absolutely no cover."

After tearing into their white ski suits, they bent down and bunched their heads together. Should they climb directly up to the hillside, to avoid being detected by the Germans rushing from Rjukan just below them on the highway? Or should they continue along the power-line road toward Rjukan until they came to the Ryes Road, which zigzagged its way beneath the cable-car lift up to Hardanger Plateau?

Idland, drugged by the realization that their chance of escape was real, jumped in with, "Let's climb straight up the mountainside from here."

But, as Helberg later wrote about this crucial moment of decision: "Poulsson and I knew the terrain and we advised against trying to climb directly up the mountainside. It would be too steep and exhausting; the moist snow on the spruce and balsam branches would be tumbling to the ground below; the foehn wind would be turning the snow already on the ground to slush. Besides, the Germans seemed more bent on reaching Vemork than searching the woods in the dark."

When the majority again agreed with the two home-town boys, they started together along the power-line road toward Rjukan, while the Germans rushed from Rjukan on the highway below them.

"Of course, going down the power-line road gave us a creepy feeling," Helberg said. "There was a good chance of our encountering Germans at any moment, but there was no other route."

"German cars and trucks kept zipping past us at great rates of speed," Poulsson added. "And that was all to the good. Those Nazis were in too much of a hurry to get to Vemork to look right or left as they raced along."

As they drew closer to Rjukan, Helberg, knowing he was only two miles from his parents' house and a hot meal, turned his eyes toward the home he vividly remembered but could not see. Were his parents awake, now that the German troop convoys had lumbered past their window? He knew they had no idea where he was, or even whether he was alive or dead. And one of the loveliest times in Rjukan, the beginning of spring, was only weeks away. Death is always more painful in the spring, and of all the kinds of grief it causes, the most distressing, the longest lasting, is the loss of a grown son or daughter. Helberg was not thinking of his own death—he was too young to believe in it—but as he trudged through the snow closer and closer to where his parents lived, he could not help thinking of what they must be going through.

When they came to a sand pit alongside the road, he led the way up through the woods toward the cable car's lower platform, which was 1,800 feet above sea level. Around another bend, the Ryes Road started zigzagging its way upward, toward the lift's top station, the control station, where the Norwegian operator lived. "It would only have been a matter of minutes to get the operator out of bed and get the cable car going," Einar Skinnarland later explained.

But so far the Germans had shown no sign that they suspected the Ryes Road might be used as an escape route. As Helberg had predicted, the alerted troops had rushed from Rjukan to Vemork and were now congregated there. The climb up the Ryes Road would take time, though, at least two hours. The men were thankful indeed when they saw that it was shrouded on each side by walls of spruce and pine.

"Once we reached the zigzag road and began to climb with our skis on our shoulders," Poulsson said, "we relaxed our efforts and felt relatively safe." Yet, with their heavy loads, it was a grueling climb, into colder and thinner air, which supplied less oxygen as their need for it increased. They had barely reached the halfway mark when a sheathing of ice began to form around their boots, ski outfits, and gloves, and on the surface of the soft snow through which they were trudging. They slipped and fell under the weight of their equipment, helped one another up with the pawing, exaggerated movements of weary men, cursed and slipped again and got up again, to struggle toward the summit and what they hoped would be escape across the mountain wastes on skis.

It took them over three hours to reach the mountain ridge leading to the plateau. When they came to a clearing, where the plateau breaks off sharply and becomes one side of the valley, Helberg shook everyone's hand and said good-by. He had to return to the cabin in Fjösbudalen for the civilian clothes he had left behind to dry.

"I'll see you all later," he said, and turned to Poulsson. "If anything happens and I'm delayed, I'll meet you a week from

today, at four in the afternoon, at the Majorstua Café in Oslo."
These two, and Haukelid and Kjelstrup, were to remain in Norway, at least until they received orders to the contrary.

"Wait, Claus," Poulsson said, "do you think . . . ?"

But before he had time to wonder aloud whether it was wise
to return to a cabin only a few miles from where the sabotage had
taken place, Helberg had pushed off on his skis and was gone.

"I skied along the ridge of the mountain overlooking the
valley," Helberg later recalled. "I could see Vemork down below
on the other side and all the German trucks and cars, with their
headlights on, congregated there. But it was still dark and I was
high above all the commotion, so I felt safe."

He reached the hut shortly after dawn, exhausted, cold, and in
need of food. The two young couples in the neighboring hut were
still there; all four of them were at the window, observing him with
great interest. They would have hot food and would gladly share
it with him; that was the Norwegian way, especially in the mountains in winter. The thought of some steaming oatmeal topped with
sugar and canned milk, a salted trout perhaps, and a mug of hot
coffee, was hard to resist. But talking to them now would be too
risky. He might say or do something, leave some traceable link that
might jeopardize the lives of the others.

As he entered the Gunnerside hut for his civilian clothes, he
remembered the syrup he had found the day before in the cupboard
—the syrup covered with dead ants.

"It was dark in the hut now, though," he said, "so when I
went to the cupboard and opened the tin, I couldn't see the ants.
I just spooned the syrup, every last bit of it, into my mouth. The
taste was all right, and I needed the energy."

After getting into dry civilian clothes and making a bundle of
his uniform for burial in the mountains, he set out on skis to join
his comrades in a cabin to the northwest by Lake Langesjå. Traveling westward about three miles, he passed the village of Turifit and

herringboned his way up the hills to the edge of the plateau, where suddenly he was hit by another of the worst storms in the history of southern Norway.

"Within seconds my map case was blown to pieces. The maps themselves were ripped from my hand and taken by the wind. I had to bury my uniform and return to Turifit, in the valley below. To move across the plateau was impossible."

Rönneberg and the others were on the plateau when they met the same storm. First, the air filled with tension and the sky with a gauzy yellow light that made everything look unreal. Then the wind changed and struck so suddenly and frigidly that the hair in their nostrils froze as hard as bits of splintered glass. Finally, as the racing clouds were sucked into the vortex of the storm, the air became thick with blinding snow, grit-laden snow that cut into their faces like a mass of stinging things with wings.

"The snow that had been too soft to walk or ski on suddenly froze to ice so hard and glassy that our skis could not take hold," Poulsson remembered. "Sliding and slipping and struggling against being bowled over by the wind, we inched our way against the gale. At times, we had to turn our heads and shoulders in order to breathe. Not a word could be spoken.

"But worse than the headwind and the difficult going was the assortment of heavy ice flakes and gravel that whirled up from the ground. It was impossible to dodge them; they hit and slashed our faces without letup. It was a miracle that no eyes were damaged."

Though the cabin by Lake Langesjå was only seven miles from where Helberg had left them at the ridge of the mountain, it took them until late afternoon to reach it. Opening the door, they pushed in and lay panting. They felt that the blood had been drained out of them. Scoured and empty, they were too exhausted to think of their accomplishment or to gain any satisfaction from it. The mission would perhaps mean something tomorrow; it meant nothing now. What meant something was that they had been through it together, not that it was over or that they had baffled and outwitted the Germans. They had changed in some important way, but they did not know how yet. There was no need to know; the change would be there, waiting for them, when they caught up with it.

Besides, they were still in Norway, on Hardanger Plateau a scant seven miles from the plant they had sabotaged. Only the storm separated them from the German search parties that were no doubt already being formed. They would have to move on, just as soon as the wind subsided.

15

When news of the Vemork sabotage reached the German High Command in Oslo (minutes after Bjårne Nilssen drove to the plant in his wood-burning motorcar), high-echelon German officers and officials immediately sped to the scene to investigate. They arrived early that morning, Sunday, February 28, 1943, while Helberg was burying his British army uniform in the mountains, and Rönneberg and the others were struggling through the storm toward their hut by Lake Langesjå.

General Wilhelm Rediess was accompanied by a battalion of tough Gestapo veterans. He led Nilssen, Chief Engineer Alf Larsen, the soldiers on duty at the time of the sabotage, and Engebretsen and Johansen, the only two men who had actually seen the saboteurs, into the plant's high-concentration room, where the wreckage around them added urgency to the inquiry. All eighteen high-concentration cells had been completely drained of their contents, and though the room was no longer the "shower room" that Larsen had found immediately after the explosion—the punctured tubes of the plant's cooling system had been bandaged—there was still plenty of water on the floor. It was ordinary water, and long before Rediess's arrival, it had washed the precious heavy water, half a ton of it, down the drains in the concrete floor on which he and the others were standing.

To make matters worse, from Germany's point of view, the expansion and modification of the high-concentration plant had been nearing completion when Rönneberg and Strömsheim had so effectively placed their explosive charges. Production had reached 150 kilograms of heavy water a month, and was expected to reach 200 kilograms in the next month. Now it would take months to clear away the damage, repair the cells, and start production again, and several more months before heavy water would be available in the high concentration needed for the German uranium research program. In short, the German Reich's scientists had suffered a delay of many months, a delay they could not afford.

General Rediess, a Hitler devotee with a love for order, accuracy, accountability, and his own skin, wanted to know what had happened, how it had happened, and why. When no one could tell him anything other than what had happened, he suppressed his rage and went through a process of elimination. The three saboteurs (he kept saying "three" because Engebretsen and Johansen had seen only three) could not have used the suspension bridge to reach the plant, he reasoned, since the two German guards on duty on the bridge would have seen anyone attempting to cross it. They could not have climbed down the mountainside by the penstocks feeding the plant, because the land mines would have blown them to pieces. They could not have crossed the gorge from the other side of the valley, because that would have been, according to his own intelligence reports, impossible. And yet the chain at the railway gate had been cut, a path had been made in the snow beside the tracks leading to and from the gate, drops of blood had been detected along the path, and a British Tommy gun had been left behind in the snow, possibly by the man who had been bleeding. How, then, did the three saboteurs, in British army uniforms, get to that railway gate on the plant's side of the gorge? Rediess wanted answers, and no one in the battered high-concentration room could supply him with even a hint of one.

The limited information he was able to gather is reflected in his report to Berlin, in which he stated: "On the night of 27th-28th February 1943, about 1:15 a.m., an installation of importance to the war economy was destroyed at the Vemork factory near Rjukan by the detonation of explosive charges. The attack was carried out by three armed men wearing grey-green uniforms.

They gained entrance to the factory by cutting a chain in the gate, and passed both German sentries and Norwegian watchmen undetected. From the effects they left behind, it can be assumed that they came from Britain."

Then, in an apparent reference to Jomar Brun's disappearance from the plant four months earlier, he added that, in his opinion, "the sabotage was a combined British Intelligence and Norwegian Resistance operation. Security police investigations are still proceeding into the matter."

These investigations included the arrest of ten of Rjukan's leading citizens, whom Rediess threatened to have shot the next day, and the arrest for questioning of some fifty of the plant's workshop and maintenance men, laboratory personnel, and shift operators.

Only the arrival on the scene of German General von Falkenhorst, a few hours later, prevented the unnecessary and unwarranted reprisals that Rediess had set in motion. Falkenhorst, Germany's surpreme military commander in Norway, saw immediately that the sabotage had been a military operation, carried out by British soldiers in uniform. He therefore ordered that the hostages be released and that no reprisals be taken against Rjukan's citizens.

Jomar Brun, whose parents had been interrogated and searched following his disappearance, later expressed deep appreciation of this action on the part of Falkenhorst. "I would like to pay tribute to the German general in command of Norway, von Falkenhorst," he said, "who against the will of the Nazi authorities decided that the action must be considered a military operation and that accordingly no steps of reprisal should be taken against the local population."

Falkenhorst called the sabotage "the finest coup I have seen in this war," and referred to the saboteurs, in a grudgingly complimentary way, as "English bandits." He was furious with the

German guards who had allowed it to happen, and went so far as to berate them in the presence of the Norwegian bystanders. Pointing toward the blasted, stainless-steel high-concentration cells, he shouted to the German commandant of the guards, "When you have a chest of jewels like this, you plant yourself on the lid with a weapon in your hand!"

Making it plain that the commandant's biggest mistake had been in not placing guards both outside and inside the high-concentration room, and at the railway gate as well, he added, "From now on there will be a guard on duty in this room and at the railway gate twenty-four hours a day."

When his continued questioning turned up the fact that the guard dogs had not been sent out on the night of the sabotage "because of the foul weather," his anger came close to making him someone else. Forbidding the guards to wear their bulky sheepskin coats while on duty, or to go about with their tunic collars turned up and their caps pulled down over their ears against the cold, he shouted, "With all those clothes on, it's no wonder you didn't hear or see the British bandits."

The commandant of the guards tried to placate him by pointing out that much had been done to protect the plant since the abortive glider attack. "Land mines were placed along the penstocks," he said. "The fence around the plant was raised and fitted with barbed wire. Machine-gun emplacements were placed on the roof of the building, along with floodlights that light up the entire area at the turn of a single switch."

"Turn the lights on!" Falkenhorst ordered.

A sergeant ran out to carry out the order. Falkenhorst waited, but no lights went on. The sergeant, recently assigned to the plant, along with several other guards, did not know where the switch was. He searched everywhere for it and finally had to ask a Norwegian workman. This explains why the floodlights were not turned on when the sirens were, immediately following the discovery of the sabotage and while Rönneberg and his men were escaping across the gorge.

Falkenhorst, even more furious, immediately signed an order sending the commandant of the guards to the Russian front. He then made up a list of changes to tighten the plant's security. The Rjukan railway station, believed to be the starting point of the saboteurs' advance upon the plant along the railway tracks, was closed to passenger traffic for the rest of the year. Roadblocks were set up along the highway leading to the plant, the mine field along the penstocks was extended, and the guard inside and outside the plant was doubled. Realizing that they now had to reckon with air attacks, the Germans camouflaged the penstocks with 800 artificial trees and installed enough smoke-screen equipment on both sides of the valley to shroud the entire plant before attacking planes arrived. The Mös dam, which supplied water to the hydro plant, was made secure with a balloon barrage and torpedo nets.

At the same time, General Rediess proclaimed a partial state of emergency in Rjukan and 11:00 P.M. curfew. A poster was put up on lampposts, bulletin boards, and in stores: "On February 28, unknown persons destroyed important apparatus in the Vemork hydro plant. In the event of similar sabotage actions, the sharpest measures will be taken against the civilian population." The town's civilian telephone exchange was shut down; telephone operations at the hydro plant were taken over by the Germans; private calls to workers at the plant were prohibited. Houses were searched, and many innocent people were arrested for various reasons. Having a piece of a fuse or a bit of dynamite lying around, as most farmers did, was reason enough to be considered dangerous to the Wehrmacht.

Up in the cabin by Lake Langesjå, Rönneberg and his men were waiting out the storm.

"What could have happened to Helberg?" Kjelstrup said, expressing what was on everyone's mind. Poulsson, especially, was hoping he would appear, for they were not only boyhood friends, but, with false identification paper, forged ration cards, and Norwegian money issued by the Bank of England, they were to go to Oslo together.

"Don't worry about Claus," he told the others in an effort to assure them as well as himself. "He's a man who can get into and out of trouble without any trouble."

After chewing on some pemmican and raisins and melting a few pieces of chocolate in their mouths, they slept through the rest of the afternoon. The storm showed no signs of abating, which meant the Germans could not have started a search of the mountains. It would be safe, they agreed, to remain in the hut until morning. But they had no choice anyway; the storm precluded travel. They slept through the night, only occasionally conscious of the buffeting wind and the granules of snow flying through crevices in the hut onto their faces.

In the morning, the first day of March, after starting just enough kindling in the stove to make hot coffee, they tried to continue on to the Cousin's Cabin, farther north, by Lake Saure. But they had gone only a few hundred yards when they were hit by a wind that seemed to increase in power the longer it lasted. Ice needles, ripped off the ground along with bits of earth and grit, tore into their faces until their cheeks felt like open wounds.

Turning their backs to the tumult, they returned to the hut, put more kindling in the stove, and waited, their growing concern for Helberg like another presence in the room. Poulsson could not help thinking that he must have met with an accident, been captured, or got himself into one of those tight situations toward which he always seemed to gravitate. Helberg knew these mountains, but could his luck hold out forever? Poulsson felt robbed of the success of the mission without his friend's being there to share it. He said nothing, though, and when the wind subsided, he agreed with Rönneberg that they had better leave some food behind for

Helberg and move on to the Cousin's Cabin. If the weather was indeed clearing, the German search parties would be starting out. An hour or two might mean the difference between escape and capture.

Nearing the Cousin's Cabin after dark, they almost missed it when Poulsson, leading the way, made a wrong turn into an inlet that drew them away from it. Quickly noticing his mistake, he waved his companions back, retraced his steps, and went the other way. Having for hours broken snow ahead of the others, he felt exhausted and disheartened, but the realization that he had to escape the Germans not only to save himself, but also to protect his mother, father, brother, and sisters, kept him going. If he was taken, dead or alive, the trail would lead directly back to Rjukan and the violent end of his family.

At the cabin, which was still carpeted and lined with the reindeer skins they had earlier used to help keep out the cold, they wasted no time in making a fire, eating, and going to sleep. The next day, March 2, when travel north had to be postponed again because of the weather, Kjelstrup and Haukelid, who were also to remain in Norway, used the time to cache away, under a huge boulder, a reserve supply of clothes, shoes, food, ammunition, and other equipment.

"After living all those weeks in the mountains, waiting for Gunnerside to arrive," Kjelstrup said later, "I realized how important it was to have reserve supplies hidden away. When the others left for Sweden, we would know the supplies were there, hidden under an innocent-looking boulder that was not going to move or be blown away. Knowing that would give us a feeling of security."

Helberg should have joined them by now, but there was still no sign of him. When he failed to appear the next day, too, they comforted themselves with the knowledge that he was a good man in the mountains and good dissembler, a man with the nerve and intelligence to talk his way out of almost any kind of tight situation.

Besides, it was not essential that he travel north with them to the headquarters hut at Lake Skryken. He knew where they were going, so he could either take another route north and rejoin them at Lake Skryken, or go directly to Oslo for his rendezvous with Poulsson a week hence.

On the third day, after leaving food behind for Helberg, they moved north again, through snow flurries too light to slow their progress. Rönneberg had already written a message for London: "High-concentration installation at Vemork completely destroyed on night of 27th-28th Stop Gunnerside on way to Sweden Stop Greetings."

When they came to a certain stone hut in the Slettedal, a valley farther north, he put the message in a coffee tin and hid the tin in a designated place to be picked up by one of the telegraphists— Einar Skinnarland or Knut Haugland—for coded transmission to London.

That same day, March 4, they reached their headquarters' hut near Lake Skryken, where the rest of their original supplies from Britain were hidden. It was here that they were to separate, and as they divided the remaining food and supplies, the emotions they were all experiencing showed in their silence and strained expressions. Rönneberg, Idland, Strömsheim, Storhaug, and Kayser packed their rucksacks, shook hands with the others, and prepared to take off, in full uniform, on their 250-mile ski trek to the Swedish border.

To avoid all contact with towns, hamlets, and farms, Rönneberg had mapped out a route that would take them through a snowbound, featureless wilderness with endless horizons, icebound valleys, barren hills, and a free-running wind fiercely hostile to human existence—an uninhabited, storm-swept world where the chances of snow blindness, exposure, and death by freezing far exceed the chances of survival. Even with maps and compasses they could lose their way, for such distinguishable landmarks as bluffs, bogs, lakes, and ravines would be under snow and therefore only vaguely outlined. The terrain, mostly a confused and baffling network of almost identical little hills and valleys, all of them rippled in the same way with wind-driven snow, could destroy a sense of direction and make it almost impossible to keep a straight compass course.

Under such conditions, would Idland, who could barely ski, slow them down enough for the Germans to outflank and encircle them? The thought was on everyone's mind as they started out, for they all knew what Idland would do in that eventuality. He had joined the mission with no expectations of ever escaping to Sweden, and, being the honorable man he was, he was not going to jeopardize the lives of the others in an effort to save his own life. If it turned out to be a race to the Swedish border between the Germans and Rönneberg's party, Idland would wish them luck, wave them on, and fend for himself.

After they skied out of sight, Poulsson, Haukelid, and Kjelstrup changed into civilian clothing and buried their uniforms a good distance from the cabin. Haukelid and Kjelstrup then packed a sledge with several sacks of food, equipment, and weapons for their five-day journey into Haukelid's own country in the northern part of the Slettedal. They would be traveling in a southwesterly direction, and on the way they would stop at Skårbu, Skinnarland's headquarters, to spend the night with him and Haugland.

"Well," Poulsson said, "now it's my turn to leave."

He shook hands with Haukelid, then turned to Kjelstrup, with whom he had spent five long months freezing, starving, and toiling in the mountains. Kjelstrup, several inches shorter, was a strong man with sloping shoulders and a face filled with understanding and kindness. Just looking at him filled Poulsson's mind with vivid memories of their days on the plateau together.

"Remember the day you carried those heavy storage batteries

through miles of fog and snow?" he asked. "You looked just like a snowman when you got back."

"I felt like one," Kjelstrup said.

"You crawled into bed with your cap pulled down over your ears and went right to sleep."

Kjelstrup smiled and nodded. "What about the time you fixed that sheep's-head soup and then dropped the kettle on the floor just as you were about to put it on the table?"

"Not a drop went to waste, though."

"No, we crawled on the floor and lapped it up."

They recalled other moments: Claus Helberg, returning bloodstained and tired from a reindeer hunt, but smiling and happy, too, with fifty kilos of meat in his rucksack; Knut Haugland, sitting hour after hour by his wireless in thirty-degree-below zero weather, with his fingers stiff and numb on the telegraph key; Einar Skinnarland, champion skier and gourmet cook, racing cross-country toward Mösstrand to obtain new information, then returning to the hut to perform the art of cooking better than any housewife. There were times when even Poulsson, the leader, felt like giving up, and it was always then that he repeated to himself a line he remembered from a book: "Hold on when there is nothing in you, except the will which says to you, Hold on!"

"Well, Arne," he said, strapping his rucksack to his back, "good-by and good luck. If we don't meet sooner, we'll meet after the war."

He stepped out, slipped on his skis, and pushed off in the direction of Oslo. He had a passport, identification cards, Norwegian money, and food stamps. Except for his pistol, which could not be traced to Britain, all military items had been discarded. He was on his own for the first time since leaving England, and instinctively, like a man afraid that he may have forgotten something, he reached inside his jacket to make sure the cyanide capsule issued to him in Scotland was still there.

The snow surface was dry, and he made good time, covering over twenty-five miles before the setting sun threw his shadow far out in front of him. An hour later, as darkness began to fall, he was close enough to the Uvdal valley to try to reach it, so he kept going in the hope of spending the night in his sleeping bag at a lower altitude. But as he started gliding down the mountainside, the lights of a small roadside inn came into view.

"I was cold and tired, and I hadn't spent a night in a warm room for months," he recalled. "Against my better judgment, I decided to get a room for the night, sit in a hot tub, and have some hot food."

Just planting his feet on the rug in the warmly lighted reception room was like returning to the Norway he remembered. A wonderful fragrance from the kitchen mixed with the aroma and crackle of burning wood in the sitting-room fireplace.

"On holiday?" the innkeeper asked with a smile.

"That's right," Poulsson said. "Good skiing."

Copies of the Quisling newspaper, *Fritt Folk,* were on sale at the counter, but that did not mean the innkeeper was a Quisling. In fact, it might mean just the opposite. Poulsson signed the register with the name on his forged passport, paid for a night's lodging, and stepped upstairs to put his rucksack in his room.

"Hungry as I was, I decided to eat first and take my bath afterwards. And I was glad I did. The food was wonderful. They served fish, potatoes, a green vegetable, and even mushrooms that had been picked the summer before and dried. Also biscuits, cheese, and jam. And real coffee."

Later, in his room, he decided to wash some underwear as well as himself. It was a great opportunity after all those grimy days in the mountains, and, besides, it was wartime, when soapy water was meant to be used twice. Sometime after his bath, while he was still half naked and his equipment was scattered all over the floor, he heard loud voices and what seemed like a disturbance downstairs. Instantly and completely the feeling of relaxation left him. He jumped from the bed and opened the door a crack to listen.

"Who is spending the night here?" asked a man with a demanding, authoritative voice.

"Just my wife and I, Sheriff," the innkeeper said, "and one guest. A man stopped by about two hours ago."

"Is he alone?"

"Yes."

"A civilian?"

"Yes. Came by on skis. Said he was on holiday."

"Let me see the register. He signed it?"

"Of course."

Poulsson closed the door and pulled on his trousers. He had left his skis and poles outside on the porch; should he climb out the window and try to escape? But his equipment, like the wreckage of his decision to spend the night at the inn, lay scattered over the room. And already there were hurried footsteps on the stairs, followed by repeated knocks on the door.

Grabbing his gun, Poulsson hid it behind his drying laundry, wondering why he had forgotten to wash his warmest pair of socks, and all the while finding time for remorse: Why didn't I spend the night in my sleeping bag?

"Who is it?"

"The police!"

As Poulsson opened the door, a huge set of teeth entered the room, pulling the sheriff's receding face behind it. He was followed by his assistant, a tall, heavy-set man with great leverage in his arms and shoulders. Poulsson looked at them with no expression, wishing he had bought a copy of *Fritt Folk* when he'd signed the register. Having it opened on the bed now would count in his favor. The sheriff was probably a Quisling; Poulsson felt this from the look in his eyes.

"Your identification," the sheriff said, his clenched smile at once hospitable and hostile.

Poulsson handed the sheriff his passport and identification cards and waited, as if trying to endure by immobility alone, while the assistant stepped around the room inspecting the scattered equipment on the floor. If he went toward the drying laundry, Poulsson would have no choice. He would have to get to the gun first and kill both of them. The gun would otherwise mean arrest, questioning, and even torture by the Gestapo, and the possible capture of his comrades.

But hanging laundry is not what one associates with a man on the run, and the gun was behind Poulsson's long underwear, the most commonplace item to be seen in Norway in winter.

"Something happened in Vemork," the sheriff said, handing Poulsson back his identification cards and passport. "Saboteurs attacked the hydro plant."

Poulsson just nodded and said, "I see." Could Kristian Kristiansen, the black-market reindeer hunter from Uvdal, have returned to town and informed the authorities? But even if he had, he would not be able to identify Poulsson. Rönneberg had seen to that by keeping Kristiansen, at all times, at least a couple of hundred yards away from Poulsson's party.

The sheriff stepped over to Poulsson's rucksack and took out his sleeping bag. Made on special order in Britain for the operation, it of course bore no marks to identify it as being British. Indeed, there would have been no need for such an insulated sleeping bag in Britain. Poulsson's boots, though, also made in Britain, were not sewn in the usual Norwegian way, and he knew that questions would start and probably lead to more questions if the sheriff noticed the difference. Luckily, the sheriff showed more interest in the sleeping bag.

"A very good sleeping bag!" he said.

"I'm on holiday. Skiing."

The sheriff and his assistant started for the door.

"Well, good hunting," Poulsson said, his excitement idling.

"No, I don't want to meet them," the sheriff said. "I hear they're armed."

As the door closed behind them, Poulsson stood there waiting for the stone in his chest to become his heart again.

"After they left," he later said, "my first thought was to get out. But I didn't, knowing that if the innkeeper saw me and informed them, the hunt would be on. So I put all my clothes on, packed everything but my wet laundry, got into bed, and went to sleep. In the morning I got up, had a hearty breakfast, and went on my way."

16

In Oslo's tightly huddled business section, where the cobblestone streets meet at all sorts of angles and the crisscrossing tram tracks gleam from steady use, the evening rush hour was in full swing. People from closing office buildings were crowding into trams and taxis, stopping at coffeehouses to meet with friends, lingering by shopwindows whose displays betrayed the paucity of goods for sale inside, or forming lines inside grocery stores, where food stamps were required for virtually every item. German soldiers on furlough, their eyes on the athletic-looking Norwegian girls in the streets, passed Jens Poulsson without interest or suspicion, some even excusing themselves as they brushed against him.

"In 1943 they had not yet turned nasty," Poulsson said later. "They wanted us to be friendly, so they were friendly. I honestly think they expected us to appreciate the fact that they had taken over our country. Of course, I knew it would all change when the war went against them, and sure enough, it did with a vengeance. In 1945 they suspected everybody. You couldn't travel about the country at all."

It was March 8, 1943, eight days after the Vemork sabotage, and he was standing beneath the clock by the underground station, across the street from the Majorstua Café, in the hope of seeing Claus Helberg. They were supposed to meet the day before, at this time, but Helberg had not shown up. Now, because Poulsson knew he could not loiter long without being asked questions, he crossed the cobblestone street beneath the trolley wires stretched above the tram tracks and peered through one of the frost-fringed windows of the café on the chance that Helberg had entered before he arrived. There, sitting at a small table with the calm familiarity of a man who visited the café at this time every day, was Helberg, with a cup of coffee to his lips.

Delighted at seeing him alive and well, Poulsson hurried in, or, rather, did everything in his power not to hurry in. "Hello, Claus," he said quietly, and sat down as though they had met that morning for breakfast.

"Try the cream puffs," Helberg said. "They're ersatz, but they at least remind you of the real thing."

When Poulsson's coffee and cream puffs were served, he moved his head closer. "When did you get in?"

"Yesterday," Helberg said. "But I met a friend of my mother's who offered to put me up in Oslo. So I couldn't make our appointment. Sorry."

"What happened to you—after you left us?"

"The storm."

Poulsson nodded. "That's what we thought."

Outside, in the gathering darkness, a crowded tram passed by on its way west into the suburbs, its trolley pole throwing off sparks where the wires intersected. The noise from the passing trams, mingled with the hubbub inside the café, made it perfectly safe to talk.

"When I reached the Langesjå hut," Helberg explained, "you had all left. I spent the night there, then moved on to the Cousin's Cabin. I thought I'd catch up with you there, but, again, you had all left. At Lake Skryken, same thing. I kept missing you by a day or two in each place."

"See anyone?" Poulsson asked.

"Not a soul. So I just skied across to Geilo and took the train to Oslo. No sign of activity anywhere."

Poulsson told him about his close call at the roadside inn, which sounded more like one of Helberg's adventures.

"What about you, Claus? Any trouble around Uvdal?"

They glanced at each other, remembering Kristiansen, who had been released by Rönneberg just before the sabotage attempt.

A whole week had passed, so Kristiansen must have returned to his home town by now. If he had talked, there would surely have been activity around Uvdal.

"No activity," Helberg said. "They haven't searched the mountains. At least not yet."

Up in Uvdal, something of great interest to the Germans was happening, and it centered around Kristian Kristiansen. After being set free in the mountains, he had continued to do what he knew how to do best—hunt reindeer. It took him a week to load his sledge with meat and ski home with the sledge in tow. He arrived in Uvdal while Helberg was on the train on his way to Oslo, and whether he delivered any of the meat to his black-market customers is not known. But shortly after his arrival, when he came upon some children in the street, he gave them what was left of the chocolate that Rönneberg had given him. Within an hour, news about "the Santa Claus with chocolate" reached the Uvdal sheriff, who did not have to be told that chocolate, not to mention chocolate made in Britain, was unobtainable in Norway in 1943. An immediate search of Kristiansen's house uncovered the reindeer meat, the fatty cuts of which he had evidently preferred to the chocolate during his journey home. Unfortunately for the man whom Rönneberg called "a man of nature, simple and harmless," the search also uncovered rifles and ammunition, which were absolutely forbidden by the German authorities.

But what interested the Gestapo more than anything else was the chocolate, which Rönneberg had naturally expected Kristiansen to consume, considering the temperature up on the plateau, long before he reached his home town. Nor did Kristiansen have any intention of betraying Rönneberg's kindness by informing on the Gunnerside party. He was simply a mountain man who preferred fat to chocolate, and also a kind man who knew children loved sweets.

The German interrogators wanted to know all about the

chocolate; they threatened and cajoled, and when Kristiansen admitted that it had been given to him by British soldiers in uniform up on the Hardanger Plateau, they could barely contain themselves. How many soldiers were there? What equipment did they have? Where on the plateau were they?

Kristiansen did not know how many soldiers there were, because he had been kept away from another group of men who may or may not have been soldiers. Their equipment was covered and lashed to a sledge, so he could not identify it. They captured him near Lake Skryken, some thirty miles from Uvdal.

The interrogators wanted details about the soldiers' uniforms, descriptions of their body builds and faces, information about the direction in which they were heading after they released him. When he told them everything he knew, they immediately informed General Rediess, who rushed by plane to Uvdal and was soon joined by General von Falkenhorst and Josef Terboven. Remembering the abortive British glider attack of the year before, they agreed that the Hardanger Plateau must have been chosen by the British as a staging area for the saboteurs. They decided to rid the vast area, once and for all, of the resistance men and British commandos infesting it, and they rolled out maps to plan their strategy.

Skinnarland, Haugland, Haukelid, and Kjelstrup were still on the Hardanger Plateau; Helberg and Poulsson were sipping coffee in the Majorstua Café in Oslo; and Rönneberg and the four men with him, one of whom could barely ski, were on the way to Sweden and freedom, though they had run into high winds and foul weather and were almost two hundred miles from their goal. All eleven of them were, of course, unaware of Kristiansen's capture by the Germans.

Indeed, Rönneberg's message confirming the success of the mission had still not been sent to London, because telegraphist Knut Haugland, after skiing to the stone hut in the Slettedal and searching in the snow for two hours, had been unable to find it.

When he returned to Skårbu, he found Haukelid and Kjelstrup there with Skinnarland. They had arrived several hours earlier and were sitting amongst all the weapons, batteries, and wireless transmitters, drinking the remains of the excellent coffee that Skinnarland had made for them.

"Where in hell did you hide the message?" Haugland said. "I couldn't find it anywhere."

Kjelstrup, who had spent five months in the mountains with Haugland, soon calmed him down.

"If *you* couldn't find it, the Germans won't find it either. But it makes no difference now anyway. Everything went according to plan. The heavy-water cells were blown up and not a shot was fired. Rönneberg and the other Gunnersides are on their way to Sweden. Poulsson is on his way to Oslo to meet Helberg."

That same evening, Haugland sent the following coded message to London:

GUNNERSIDE OPERATION CARRIED OUT WITH COMPLETE SUCCESS ON NIGHT OF 27TH-28TH FEBRUARY STOP HIGH CONCENTRATION PLANT COMPLETELY DESTROYED STOP NO SUSPICIONS AROUSED AND NO SHOTS EXCHANGED STOP GREETINGS.

Meanwhile, preparations were being speeded by the Germans for a vast man hunt of the plateau's 3,500 square miles. An urgent call was sent to every German garrison in Norway for soldiers who could ski. Quisling police went from door to door to requisition skis, ski poles, and ski outfits from Norwegian residents in neighboring towns. Over 10,000 German troops were ordered rushed to strategic points in order to seal off the whole of Hardanger Plateau. Planes flew reconnaissance flights; trucks and even tanks began lumbering into nearby staging areas.

The German-controlled news agency in Oslo said that "it had long been rumored that British parachutists had made the mountain area their headquarters for launching sabotage raids against the adjacent industrial establishments." This led to rumors throughout southern Norway that "eight hundred British paratroopers" had landed on the plateau and were engaged in a "fierce battle" against German security forces "directed by SS-General Rediess himself."

But in all of Norway, the only men in British army uniforms were Rönneberg and the four men under him, and though they were still up on the plateau, they were now approaching the northeast corner of it.

"We had appalling weather conditions and could not make good time," Rönneberg recalled. "We took only what food supplies we thought we'd need, but we were still soldiers in uniform, in accordance with the strict orders laid down in London, and our guns, ammunition, and other military equipment added to the weight we had to carry. It was absolutely necessary weight, though, for we knew we might encounter German soldiers at any moment."

Quiet Kasper Idland, the one man who did not believe they would escape to Sweden, was "extraordinarily willing and good humored during our retreat," according to Rönneberg. "He tried very hard to keep up with us. He kept struggling to keep up, but never complained, never asked us to slow down. If we had left him behind, he would not have called after us. We knew that, but of course we had no intention of leaving him behind."

Every night when they stopped to sleep, each man chewed his ration of raisins and pemmican, removed his boots, slipped them in his sleeping bag (so they would not freeze and become filled with snow during the night), then crept into the bag himself. Even when no snow was falling, the wind unfailingly blew snow around and on top of them, until in the morning they resembled five white mounds. They did not mind this, for the snow on top of them acted as a kind of quilt against the cold. The snow beneath them, though, was another matter. It always tended to melt from the warmth of their bodies, seep into their sleeping bags, and dampen their backs, or sides, if they shifted position during the night. Before long, after sweating through each day and trying in vain to dry out at night, their sleeping bags and boots began to smell as bad as they did. Only the ammonia-sharp air, which luckily surrounded each and every one of them, acted as an antidote.

"We crossed five broad valleys along the way," Rönneberg said, "but saw no German troops and succeeded in avoiding contact with the civilian population. It took us eighteen days to reach the great forests that mark the beginning of the Swedish frontier. We spent the night there in our sleeping bags, and the next morning we undressed, discarded our uniforms and all military equipment—boots, underwear, windproof pull-overs, guns, and ammunition—and put on the civilian clothes we had brought with us from Britain.

"Our cover story for the Swedish authorities was that we had been part of an illegal cell, building houses for the Germans. I had been cell leader, and the others did not know the details. They had simply been told by me that they had to get away."

The story worked all right in the beginning, but as they were questioned by more and more officials, some suspicion was aroused by the similarity of their equipment. Their skis, poles, and boots were almost identical; their civilian trousers and jackets appeared to be, and in fact were, cut by the same tailor from the same bolt of cloth. That five men should have such homogeneous taste was ludicrous, but the Swedish authorities, lenient toward anyone trying to escape occupied Norway, accepted their story and sent them to a refugee camp.

"I asked for a three-day leave and went to Stockholm with the idea of contacting the British Embassy," Rönneberg said. "Entering Stockholm at night, after the London blackouts and bombings, was an amazing experience. All the city's lights were on; there were lighted buses and restaurants everywhere. I went to the opera the first night. *La Traviata.* I had to pinch myself to believe it."

At the British Embassy the next day, he asked to see the military attaché. When his turn came, he walked in and gave his name.

"Why did you come here?" the attaché asked. Rönneberg's name told him nothing, though the outcome of the Gunnerside mission had been eagerly awaited in both London and Washington. After several checks and telephone calls, Rönneberg's identity as the leader of the Gunnerside operation was corroborated. This led to covert preparations for the release of the others from the refugee camp and their return by plane to Britain.

"Before leaving Sweden we bought all new skiing and camping equipment, compasses, sleeping bags, extra woolens and so forth, in preparation for our next assignment from Britain to Norway. The biggest thrill of all, though, for me, was our return to Britain, which I considered my second home. In fact, during the operation, we always talked about going home—to Britain. And yet, while in Britain, we always talked about going home—to Norway."

17

It was shortly after Rönneberg and his men reached Sweden that the sweeping search of Hardanger Plateau by the Germans started. The two telegraphists, Skinnarland and Haugland, learned of it through one of Skinnarland's contacts and decided at once to get themselves and their radio equipment out of their cabin in the Hamrefjell mountains and move to higher altitudes.

"When we learned of the magnitude of the *Razzia*," Skinnarland recalled, "we cleared out our things . . . and advised London that we were moving into more inaccessible parts of the mountains and staying in a tent until the raid was over. We had food and the paraffin to cook it, and pitched the tent in the steepest part of the mountain above Skinevain, about halfway between the farm at Hamaren, where my two loyal contacts were Jon Hamaren and his sister Birgit, and the farm of Skindalen, where Olav Skindalen and his family, in spite of their meager livelihood, unfailingly supported my comrades and me with food, transmittal of messages, and companionship. Haugland and I did some reconnaissance with binoculars from the surrounding mountain peaks, which we had access to without making tracks in the snow. We observed a couple of the German patrols proceeding up Lake Mösvann, but thanks to the excellent intelligence work of my farmer friends and their buffering, Haugland and I had no close calls. Except for a visit by a Fiesler Storch plane, the German search parties at no time came close to our hiding place. . . ."

Haukelid and Kjelstrup, also up in the high altitudes during the raid, had less food and only raw wood to heat it with. "We were so high up in the mountains," Kjelstrup has said, "that we had to travel several miles to the nearest bush. Even then, the junipers we dug from the snow and hauled back produced very little heat. I honestly believe we created more heat by hauling it back than by burning it. I remember I even had dreams about wood at night, dry wood, the way Poulsson had dreams about reindeer meat, hot, fatty reindeer meat, before he bagged that reindeer in time for Christmas."

They, too, avoided capture, because the Germans used too many men, 10,000, to find a total of four men, on a 3,500-square-mile plateau made up of countless hills, rivers, lakes, moors, and marshes. Nor were the Germans aware that they were trying to find only four men. Having heard the rumors about the landing of 800 British saboteurs on the plateau, they kept looking for companies of men, or at least platoons. They wasted thousands of gallons of fuel trying to track down the saboteurs with airplanes, some of which dropped bombs and one of which crashed. Even Reich Commissar Josef Terboven took part in the search, until his aircraft made a forced landing and he had to be rescued by his own men.

The two opposing forces were, therefore, ill matched in a way that favored the four hunted men. German ski patrols were everywhere, searching all the cabins and burning every one they found containing arms. They made so many ski tracks in the snow that it soon became impossible to distinguish their own from those their quarry might have made. They actually began to shoot at one another, they were so unfamiliar with the snowy terrain and the distortion of vision it created. Instead of living in the mountains as their quarry did, surreptitiously, with all their senses alert, looking for evidence of the presence of others and never exposing themselves for long to the chance of being seen, they skied roughshod over snow that contained clues they never noticed.

It was Claus Helberg's bad luck, or his incorrigible tendency to get into trouble, that prompted him to return from Oslo while the German search of Hardanger Plateau was in progress.

"My job after the sabotage was to go back to the Rjukan area to be at the disposal of the Milorg there. I took the train to the Uvdal valley with the intention of skiing the rest of the way to Rjukan. I had heard nothing about the German raid, and everything looked normal as I set out across the plateau on skis."

Helberg knew that many Norwegians considered the plateau alien, unfriendly territory, and indeed there was, even on the fairest days, something implacable about its overpowering sky, something sinister about its desolation, its profound and unearthly silence. But for five months it had been his home, and now he loved it. Like the town of Rjukan itself, it had become a part of him, a place he would gravitate back to for as long as he lived.

After skiing over thirty miles from Uvdal, he reached the cabin at Lake Skryken and started to enter it for some rest and something to eat. The door was unlocked, and the moment he stepped in he saw that someone had been there, someone unfriendly. Table and chairs had been thrown aside, bunks searched, mattresses cut, cupboards and drawers broken into, and food taken.

Under the circumstances, the wreckage was a stunning thing to see, for not once during his months on the plateau had he come upon a single reminder that his country was occupied. He had taken the plateau's isolation and remoteness so much for granted that the enemy's existence on it now seemed almost unfair—at once unbelievable and demanding of belief.

Maybe they're still in the area, he thought, and ran outside to scan the surrounding mountains. To the east, less than half a mile away, were five German soldiers skiing toward the cabin with the wild impetus of men after a murderer of children. They had obviously seen him enter and were attempting to surround him.

"My only weapon was a Colt .32, so I could hardly put up a fight," Helberg said later. "I had to rely on my skis, and in a matter of seconds I had them on and pushed off. They had not managed to surround me. There was an open gap I thought I could get through, so I headed that way, into the sun, to make myself a difficult target. I was not very scared, but when they started shooting, I thought, This is the end for me, though I remember I was glad we had succeeded at Vemork."

The Germans, shooting at him into the sun, kept missing. A second or two later, the shooting stopped. He glanced around and saw that they had decided to try to overtake him instead.

"Here we were," he said, "in the mountains of Telemark, where competitive skiing was born, and now the competition was for my own life."

Good skiing poles give a little whip that helps push a skier forward, and Helberg had not only good bamboo poles, but also excellent Nordic skis, which gave him a powerful forward thrust. Picking his route into the sun, he surveyed the untracked snow in the distance to see which turn would be to his advantage, which hill might conceal a slight change of direction on his part. He also kept glancing backward to see if they were gaining on him. Would he have time to swallow his suicide capsule if he made a bad turn and fell? As the race continued, past frozen waterfalls and ravines, around craggy butts, frosted bits of vegetation, and huge solitary rocks sculptured by the wind, it was as if he were being pursued as much by a fear to use the capsule as by the Germans. The suspense kept increasing; it made him want to use his body in some new, impossible way, as he dug his poles into the crusted snow in a desperate effort to impel himself forward faster.

After about an hour, three of the Germans began to lose ground. One by one they tapered their efforts until finally, as if by mutual consent, they stopped altogether. But the other two had lost no ground at all. They kept up with him long after the other three had disappeared behind the intervening hills and valleys. Not until another ten miles had been covered did one of the remaining two become exhausted, or suffer a muscle strain or cramp, and stop.

"So now there was just the one chasing me," Helberg said,

"and he was fresher than I, and a good skier, too. So the race went on, for another hour, maybe two hours."

During these grueling hours, the distance between them never changed by more than thirty or forty yards. At one moment Helberg would be gaining on him, the next moment the German would be gaining on Helberg. But Helberg had put in over thirty miles before the race started; he was much closer to exhaustion than the German, who appeared determined, with his forward-leaning stance and his head thrust out in front of him, to see the race through to the end. All Helberg could do was go on until he could go on no longer—until his legs, arms, or heart gave out and he collapsed. He was always about to reach this point, it seemed, just about to, but somehow, though he was never conscious of driving himself, he never did. Whenever he approached a hill, he did not decide, so much as sense, which skiing technique to use to climb it. Without a second's hesitation, he either herringboned, side-stepped, used the traverse–side-step combination, or simply skied straight up with the aid of his poles, as though his skis were an extension of his feet and did not have to be "told" what to do.

It was while he was struggling up a hill, panting for breath and straining every muscle, that his mind grasped something vitally important: every time he climbed a hill, he gained ground on his pursuer; every time he glided down a hill, he lost ground to his pursuer.

"I therefore tried to find as many hills to climb as I could," Helberg said, "until finally I went as high as I could and there were no more hills to climb, only hills to descend. I started down, pushing off with all my strength, trying to use every twist and turn to my advantage, but after about a quarter of an hour I could hear his skis and poles behind me. He got closer and yelled 'Hands Up!' in German."

Had his pursuer, whose only weapon was a Luger, known that Helberg had a gun, he might have shot him in the back. He was close enough to try, but he had obviously wanted all along to bring Helberg back alive for questioning. This must have been his intention, for as Helberg turned, the German suddenly straightened, his spine like a spear in his head, at the sight of the Colt in Helberg's hand. They were about forty yards apart, with Helberg on slightly lower ground and the setting sun shooting rays upward from the mountain peaks far to the west behind him.

"I realized that the man who emptied his magazine first would lose, so I fired once—and missed. After that I held my fire and stood there as a target at forty yards' range. In a few seconds it would be all over. I would be either dead or alive—or wounded, in which case I would immediately bring on death by swallowing my suicide capsule."

The German was so infuriated, or frightened, by the summons to fight that he immediately fired back, also missing, as Helberg's stomach froze. He fired again, the bullet boring its deadly tunnel through the air alongside Helberg's ear. This is it, Helberg thought, as the German aimed and fired again, and missed again. From hunting reindeer, Helberg knew that it was very difficult to shoot accurately in the mountains like this, into rays of sunlight that distort the snowy landscape and the distances between objects. The German probably also had sweat in his eyes, and all kinds of carry-over tensions in his muscles from skiing so long. This steadied Helberg, helped him to believe the next bullet would miss its mark, too. But should he move an inch or two to either side? Would it help? Or would it change his luck? Standing there erect and still, he did not have to decide. The next bullet went spinning past his arm, close enough to have hit him if he had moved in that direction by two inches.

All he wanted then, before the German fired a fifth time, was his life, and he had a gun in his own hand, with his finger tight against the trigger. The hardness of it kept sending messages to his brain to aim and shoot back, just as his enemy was doing. His life was hanging on chance, but he resisted even as the German shot again, and missed again. There was now just one bullet left in the

German's gun, and everything in Helberg was shaking. He probably would not have been able to shoot even if he had decided to —but again he did not have to decide. The last bullet came close enough for him to hear, then glanced off a rock behind him with a sharp ping.

Suddenly everything was right; it could not have been better. Their roles were reversed. Helberg still had five bullets in his Colt .32, and the German none in his Luger. And since they had been going downhill when the German overtook him, they would be going uphill now. Helberg was better going uphill; he knew it and so did the German, who quickly, in an effort to get out of range, swung about and started back in his tracks up the hill. If he reached the top and started down the other side without being shot, he would be free. There would be too many hills to go down for him to be overtaken, and besides, Helberg would not dare chase him back to his armed comrades.

"I hesitated a second or two, then went after him as fast as I possibly could," Helberg recalled. "Every second counted. His comrades might turn up over one of the hills at any moment."

Helberg did not have to contend with the distorting rays of the setting sun; they were behind him, aiding rather than hindering his vision of the German's broad back. But he was no longer sure of his concentration after the pressure of standing there as a target. Do it, shoot, he told himself. Do it. He's as close now as he'll ever be. But he got around the urge just by noticing the German's frantic movements. I'm a better climber, he thought, I can get close enough to make the bullets count.

He kept gaining, little by little; the German knew it and he knew it, and that made him a better climber than ever, and the German not as good a climber as before. They were approaching the top of the hill, and just before the German reached it, Helberg stopped in his tracks and fired, aiming at the German's middle, the bull's-eye at the small of the back, to give himself room for error in every direction.

"From a distance of about thirty yards, I fired several shots at him. He began to stagger and finally stopped, hanging over his ski sticks, like a man on crutches. I turned around and pushed on to get away before the others came. The sun was setting. It would soon be dark. I was safe, at least for the time being."

But his ski tracks posed a problem, for even in the dark the Germans would be able to follow them. Luckily, he knew of a nearby lake, Vråjoen, where there was more than enough bare ice to conceal his tracks, so he headed in that direction. The night was clear and still, but moonless and dark. His exhaustion, made worse by the nervous tension of standing as a target, showed in exaggerated movements and careless turns. Just north of the lake, he was skiing along the edge of a ravine when it occurred to him that the German had actually fired all six of his shots in rapid succession, not with a time span between, as he had thought. Not more than a second could have separated one shot from the next; it had all happened that fast. The time span between shots had been illusory.

He was thinking of this, and of how close he had been to death, when he sailed off a cliff, falling over 120 feet, to a snowy incline below.

"It was quite an air journey," he later recalled, "but it was not until I stopped sliding and rolling and came to a stop in a snowdrift that I thought I might be hurt."

For hours he had been panting with exertion, trying to pull the air into his lungs, and now, too tired to move, and too encumbered with snow to try to, he waited carefully for the pain to come and say what it had to say. Starting in his left shoulder, it ran through his left arm. Bone must be broken, he decided, because when he tried to move the arm something foreign happened all the way down to his wrist. Oh, it's broken, all right, he thought, when he looked at it. So he sat there, catching his breath and thinking and looking up at the cliff he had fallen over. He was alone, injured, and still in an area where he might run into an-

other German patrol or be overtaken by the one he had just out-
run. He had his gun and additional ammunition, but one gun
would mean nothing against five, and with a broken arm he could
forget about trying to escape.

Rising to his feet slowly and painfully, he was relieved to
find that nothing had happened to his legs. His skis, too, were un-
damaged, and if he traveled at a reasonable pace and concentrated
on what he was doing, he could manage with one ski pole. Besides, he had to take the chance. Only a doctor could help him
now.

Early the next morning, after reaching Mogen, at the northern tip of Lake Mös, he barely escaped five German soldiers by
ducking behind some scrub as they came up a path along which
he was traveling. A major search was under way; the place was
swarming with Germans. All the same, he could not take to the
mountains again with an injured shoulder, a broken arm, and no
food. He had to get to a doctor, so he continued south to Hamaren
farm, near where Lake Mös broadens out to become a small
inland sea. He, too, knew the people at the farm, the Hamarens,
two of the most dedicated anti-Nazis in southern Norway, and
good friends of Einar Skinnarland.

"The farmers in the mountains during the war were absolutely fantastic," Skinnarland says today. "Being natural poachers
when it comes to reindeer, they seem to develop natural abilities
in espionage."

Jon and Birgit Hamaren, from the beginning of the German
occupation, had aided the resistance by cunningly planning local
counterintelligence operations, concocting cover stories to prevent
gossip, and furnishing facilities such as the hunting cabin used by
Skinnarland and Haugland to send messages to London.

When the Hamarens told Helberg that the Germans were
searching every farmhouse in the area, he stayed only long enough
to gulp down some food and stuff his pockets with more. After

thanking them, he skied across Lake Mös, easing himself along with one ski pole, and continued south to Rauland, the largest town in the area. He had been on his feet for thirty-six hours and had covered a distance of 112 miles. The long chase, the duel in the snow, and the fall off the cliff seemed to have made cereal of his body's fiber. He felt weak and dreamy and could barely tense his muscles.

In Rauland he ran into the biggest concentration of enemy troops and Gestapo agents since leaving Oslo. "There was a great deal of commotion," he said. "I couldn't have picked a worse place of refuge. Terboven and Rediess had just been there to inspect the troops, which numbered over 300 men. To make matters worse, the weather had suddenly turned mild and warm, making it impossible to move on. I went to the home of a shopkeeper I knew and got myself a place to sleep on the kitchen floor. The bedrooms were occupied by German officers ordered to the area for the ongoing search of the mountains."

Helberg decided the next day to put his imagination and guile to work. He became an impostor. He went directly to the Germans, and to the first one who could speak Norwegian, an army sergeant, he introduced himself as a local man, presented his London-forged identity card, and explained that as someone who knew the area, he had volunteered to join the Germans in their search for the Vemork saboteurs. Unfortunately, after breaking his arm in the mountains while on duty, he had been forced to return for medical treatment.

"The Germans evidently thought I was a nice chap," Helberg said. "What they would have done if they had known I was one of the saboteurs they were looking for, I still shudder to think about."

The German sergeant not only believed him, but also immediately ordered two soldiers to take him to the field doctor, with instructions that the shoulder and arm be treated. This would mean that Helberg would have to undress, at least to the waist, and that while doing so he would somehow have to hide his gun. He recalled Leif Tronstad's admonition in Britain that SOE did not want heroics from its agents, and decided that even if he were caught with the gun, he would try to talk rather than shoot his way to freedom.

Since complete concealment was out of the question, he simply slipped the gun into his jacket pocket and hung the jacket with his other clothes in the doctor's office. "Oh, that," he was going to say if someone noticed it, "well, you see, as guide to the German patrol in the mountains, I was allowed to use it." But he acted innocent enough, and showed enough genuine pain from his injury, not to attract the attention of anyone.

After being bandaged and given a shot and some follow-up tablets to kill the pain, he was told to get dressed by the doctor, who luckily stepped outside for a moment to make arrangements for Helberg to be taken by ambulance to Dalen, farther south. By the time the doctor returned to explain the arrangements he had made, Helberg was dressed and ready to go, with his gun hidden from view.

"From Dalen I was to make my own way to Oslo for treatment, and when the ambulance dropped me off, I bid my helpers *Auf Wiedersehen* and walked away with my skis and poles over my good shoulder."

The boat for Oslo was not to leave until the following morning, so Helberg, in great need of rest, headed straight for the hotel in town. The Bandak Tourist Hotel was an attractive place, and he was given a room in the main building on the second floor. But no sooner had he hidden his gun, under the downy quilt that one finds in winter on every hotel bed in Norway, than the hotel began to reverberate with voices and the stamping of boots. Terboven and Rediess had arrived, and their staffs were in the process of requisitioning rooms.

"I was interrogated and required to show my identification card and explain the purpose of my stay in Dalen, as were all the other guests, about thirty altogether," Helberg recalled. "My identification card was carefully examined and found to be in perfect order. Perhaps for that reason, and because of my injury, I was allowed to retain my room."

Having no intention of hiding in his room, he went downstairs to see whether there might be a chance of escaping. There were Germans everywhere, guards at every exit, and pointed questions were being asked of anyone trying to leave for whatever reason. Biding his time, he ambled into the sitting room and sat down in a large soft chair among other Norwegian guests.

"Get up! You cannot sit there," a German official said. "That chair is reserved for Reich Commissar Josef Terboven."

Helberg rose to his feet, went to the dining room, chose a table too small and too close to a sideboard stacked with dishes and utensils to be reserved for Terboven, and sat down.

"I remember having a fine dinner of fried trout, small boiled potatoes dotted with dehydrated parsley, baby carrots braised in reindeer fat, and crusty, homemade bread with a strong, smelly Norwegian cheese rich in protein and vitamins. The wild strawberries, picked the previous summer and preserved, were served on a sweetened bun the size of an American silver dollar, with coffee. The reason I remember the meal is simple. I really needed the food, and that made eating it almost an emotional experience."

While he was drinking his coffee something else happened that made the meal an experience. Terboven and Rediess and their party came in and occupied two large tables by the fire. After being served wine, they ordered a beautiful young Norwegian girl at another table to dine with them. She at first refused, then, under pressure, joined them with an unsmiling, defiant expression. Her name was Åse Hassel, and she spoke perfect German. This delighted Terboven and Rediess, until she told them, in German, that her father was a colonel in the Royal Norwegian Army. "He is in England," she added, "and I am proud of it." This of course meant that he had escaped during the German takeover of Norway and would be returning to help rid his country of the Nazis. Later, when she laughed with scorn at the suggestion that she go up to one of the bedrooms with them, they reddened with anger and ordered her to leave.

Early the next morning, eighteen of the Norwegian guests were ordered to pack and be prepared to leave the hotel in ten minutes. Åse Hassel and Claus Helberg were among them. When they had all assembled in the lobby, they were told that they were being arrested because of their "impertinent attitude" toward the Reich Commissar. They were to be taken to Grini concentration camp for questioning and possible internment and would be leaving as soon as the bus arrived.

"I was very much in doubt as to my next move," Helberg said later. "Should I tell Terboven and company the same story I had told the Germans at Rauland, or would that only make things stickier, now that I was among the arrested? There would probably be less risk in going along in the bus with the other prisoners. The ride to Grini would take many hours; the bus would have to stop along the way; I could escape. I certainly could not stay with the transport all the way to Grini—not with my gun tucked away inside my ski jacket."

While waiting in the lobby with the others, he was relieved to see Terboven and Rediess leave the hotel and speed away in army vehicles with their entourage of assistants and guards. A little later, a big bus pulled up in front of the hotel, whereupon the prisoners were escorted down one by one. Helberg made sure he was the last one, in an effort to get a seat close to the door. Unfortunately, the German in charge of the loading interpreted his delaying tactics as a reluctance to board the bus, or, worse, an attempt to escape. He kicked Helberg from behind with such force that he went headlong down the hotel steps. In an effort to cushion his fall, he threw out his uninjured arm. As he did so, his Colt slipped loose from his jacket and fell, scraping along the pavement until it came to a stop between the booted legs of another German.

Helberg got to his feet wondering why nothing that happened to him ever happened first in his imagination. The German's boots were so much shinier than he would ever have imagined them to be, with so much snow and slush about. And his Colt—it seemed suddenly to share with the shiny boots some kind of essential relationship in which authority, evidence, guilt, and conviction all became one.

This is not happening to me, he told himself. It's too far-fetched. I'm imagining it.

But the gun was still there, between the shiny boots, and now the German was picking it up and looking at it. If it were traced to the shooting in the mountains, he would be summarily executed.

"As you can see," he said in broken German, "it is not loaded."

He had that relaxed look of belonging anywhere he happened to be, especially when he was in trouble. His nervous exhaustion and broken arm also came to his aid, for he might otherwise have tried to escape. As it was, the mishap became just another in a series of mishaps toward which he would have to be philosophical if he was to survive.

Everything depended upon what they decided to do with him, and being low-echelon German soldiers, trained to take, rather than give, orders, they could not decide. That alone was reason for hope; had Terboven and Rediess been there to inspect the recently fired gun and interrogate Helberg about it, there would have been little doubt about his fate. But the German guards, unaccustomed to making decisions, argued with one another instead. One wanted him put under guard at the hotel until someone higher in command was informed; the other said that orders were orders and that their orders were to take everyone to Grini. The decision on what to do with him could be made by the officer in charge at Grini. All they had to do was turn him in with a report that he had had a gun in his possession.

When they finally decided to take him with them, he was told to get to the back of the bus, where all the seats were taken and he was forced to sit on his rucksack in the aisle on the floor. One armed German guard sat in the front of the bus; four armed guards, with two motorcycles, each with a side passenger cabin, escorted the bus front and rear. The chance of his escaping with a broken arm before the bus arrived at Grini was too remote to contemplate. Instead, with his built-in resiliency, he contented himself with the thought that the farther he was taken from where he had shot the German in the mountains, the less chance there would be of his gun being traced.

Looking around at those near him in the bus, he was delighted to find, in the seat beside him, Åse Hassel. She was intelligent as well as pretty, friendly without being flirtatious, and only a few years younger than the lean, twenty-four-year-old Helberg. It took them no time at all to enter into a lively conversation about everything that entered their minds. They laughed and joked together like people going on a picnic rather than to a concentration camp. To everyone else in the bus, and especially to the German guard up front, their animation was utterly incompatible with the trouble they were in. Besides being the only ones in the bus talking, in time they became the center of everyone's attention, a veritable pocket of gaiety.

Finally, the German guard strode back and stood over them as if trying to convince himself, as well as them, that this was German-occupied Norway and not Norwegian-occupied Germany.

"What are you two doing?"

"Doing?" Åse Hassel said. "Doing? What do you mean?"

That she spoke perfect German seemed only to add to his confusion. "Stop the nonsense, that's all."

"Are we not allowed to talk?" she continued in the educated German he had been taught to respect.

Without answering, the guard strode back to his seat up front. This prompted Åse Hassel to make some amusing comment about her confrontation with Terboven the night before. When this resulted in more laughter, the German guard stomped back and stood over them again.

Helberg, recalling the incident, said: "Once he knew the girl spoke German, he became envious as well as angry."

"Go up to the front of the bus," he said to Helberg. "Take my seat. And you go forward, too," he said to the older person sitting next to Åse Hassel. "From now on, I will sit here."

On his feet, with his rucksack over his shoulder, Helberg nodded to Åse Hassel and said *Auf Wiedersehen* with a special emphasis that he hoped she would interpret correctly. He even waved good-by to her, behind the German's back, as an added signal that he was going to try to escape, and from her eyes he thought, or believed he had reason to hope, she got the message. If so, she would engage the guard's attention by talking to him in German.

"It was an old-fashioned bus, with a door controlled by the driver via a big lever," Helberg said. "Luckily, I was now in the seat nearest the door, and the Norwegian driver paid no attention to me. He kept his eyes on the road and maintained the same speed as the lead motorcycle, which continued at a steady pace about fifteen yards ahead of us. The motorcycle in the rear maintained the same speed from about the same distance, so there would be very little room for error when I made my move."

Helberg sat there, tension like a compress against his temples, as the cold air seeping through the front of the bus crowded round his ankles. If he waited too long, the German guard might come back and reclaim his seat. And yet if he jumped before the bus came to some roadside cover, the guards in the motorcycles would have no trouble shooting him. As they started slowly up the steep hills at Lier, he strained his eyes, waiting for a place where the woods came close to the road. He knew he could not be too particular, for they were already close enough to Grini for the German guard, whom Åse Hassel was entertaining in the rear, to come forward.

When they came to the top of one of the hills and he saw that woods and road were separated by only a narrow field, he decided to wait no longer. With a momentary thought for Åse Hassel that was like a prayer, he stood up, grabbed and pulled the lever before the driver knew what was happening, and, "pursued by a torrent of abuse from the startled German guard in the rear," jumped out and fell on the road. There were shouts and screeches of brakes as the bus and both motorcycles came to a stop. The two guards in the rear motorcycle, who were closest to him because of their forward movement before jamming on their brakes, were just about to pounce on him alongside the road when he sprang to his feet and started across the field, running with all his might between flashlight beams and the thuds of bullets hitting the ground around him. Taking advantage of every scrap of cover, breaking stride and changing both speed and direction, to prevent them from steadying their aim, he just managed to reach the edge of the woods when hand grenades began exploding around him. He hit the ground as stones and bits of flying dirt snapped and ripped at him from all directions. He got up and ran, and hit the ground again, always mindful of getting deeper into the woods between one explosion and another. As he gained the shelter of the big timber, he was startled by the thump of one of the grenades against his shoulder. Bolting away, he plunged into the pine brush and lay there, wild-eyed, waiting for it to explode. It should have blown his head and shoulder off. If not that, it should have riddled him with shrapnel as he went flying through the air to get away from it. But either it had been a dud or the German soldier, in his excitement, had forgotten to pull the pin.

He could have lain there for hours, or at least until he stopped trembling, but because he could still hear the guards talking, he slowly struggled back into doing something. Through a web of twigs and fallen branches, he held all five of them within his line of vision as they started back through the field toward their vehicles. At the same time, he kept checking with his mind the condition of his body. Had anything happened to him? Was he bleeding without knowing it? Because just being alive after what had happened was deserving of attention, too. It was like noticing the still-turning wheels of a car after the car has plunged off a cliff and landed on its back. His wheels were still turning, and he could hardly believe it. I'm all right, I think, he said to himself as his panting subsided. I'm all right, he repeated to himself, I'm all right!

The guards were preparing to move on. At Grini, to the officer in charge, they would say that a prisoner attempting to escape had been mortally wounded and that a search of the wooded area in daylight would uncover his body. To those in the bus they would say the same thing, to make the story generally accepted before they reached Grini and the prisoners were questioned. As the convoy moved on, Helberg could not help thinking of Åse Hassel, at the rear of the bus, suffering unnecessary regret and remorse at what she would have to think was the failure of their impromptu stratagem.

Helberg had no skis, no gun, and no food, and his shoulder and arm ached with a pain he tried in vain to ignore. Yet he had to get away before the officer in charge at Grini dispatched soldiers from the camp to search for him. Struggling to his feet, he plowed through the heavy snow beside the road rather than risk the chance of ambush. There was very little light filtering down from the sky, but as he pushed on, mile after mile, and the irises of his eyes widened, he saw, or thought he saw, up ahead on his side of the road, a darkened farmhouse. It looked deserted, but in Norway after nightfall in winter, especially during the war, every house looked deserted. He knew he was taking a chance, but he did it anyway—tapped on the window, three times, then a fourth time for good measure. After waiting a minute or so, he tapped again. He was exhausted, hungry, and cold, so he tapped once more. I'll try the door, he thought, when suddenly he saw someone peering at him from the darkened interior of the house. A light went on, and the door swung open.

He entered into the warmth of a Norwegian welcome—food and drink, a bed, and no embarrassing questions. The next day the farmer summoned a Norwegian doctor, who also asked no questions. Helberg, the man who knew how to get into and out of trouble, was taken to the Drammen hospital in an ambulance while German soldiers were searching for him in the woods along the road where he had escaped from the bus. After being treated at the hospital, he was transferred to Lier Asylum and put in a solitary cell as a "dangerous lunatic" until his arm and shoulder healed. Now and then he saw an enemy soldier or two through the barred window, but because he was in a cell block for violent patients, he was bothered by no one during his three-week stay. At last, with borrowed skis and poles and a small rucksack of food, he made his way to Sweden, and from there to Britain, where Rönneberg and the others welcomed him as brothers might have a wayward and troublesome member of the family.

18 When Helberg arrived in Britain, experts in London were still busy assessing the damage done to the Vemork plant by the successful Gunnerside raid. Basing their estimates on the fact that it takes over a year for the whole electrolytic process, starting with ordinary water and ending with heavy water, to go through its various stages, they decided that heavy-water production had been set back about two years. Not only had the high-concentration cells in the last and most time-consuming stage of the process been destroyed, but also the high-concentration heavy water itself had escaped down the drains. The Germans could repair the damage and rebuild the high-concentration cells, but until those cells were filled again, drop by drop, with water from preceding stages in the process, there would be no high-concentration heavy water.

The Germans, though, worked day and night on the problem, and on July 8, 1943, five months after the Gunnerside raid, Einar Skinnarland, who had set up a radio station powered by a makeshift water wheel up on Hardanger Plateau, reported to London that Vemork was expected "to reach full production of heavy water again from August 15th, 1943." The Germans had accomplished this, Skinnarland explained in another message, by bringing some of the heavy water they had already taken from the plant back from Germany and filling the emptied heavy-water installations with it so that the whole process in all its stages could be started again. On August 3, 1943, he reported that "partial production of the 99.5% heavy-water concentrate started in June" and that "the output has now reached 4.5 kilos [about 10 pounds] per day."

During this period, there were exchanges between London

and Skinnarland about "sabotaging the production by adding small amounts of vegetable oil to the distillation vats." London requested that this be tried without endangering the security of the contacts inside the plant.

On August 9, Skinnarland reported that "the daily production at times had been reduced to 1.5 kilos [about 3 pounds] as a result of adding oil to the distillation vats."

These sabotage efforts did not, however, satisfy General Leslie Groves, in Washington, especially after he learned that shipments of heavy water from Vemork to Germany were now being made under very heavy guard. That these shipments were irreducibly small only added to Groves's determination to have them stopped altogether. What better evidence was there that the Germans were close to solving their uranium problem than the protection they were giving every pound of heavy water extracted from the Vemork plant?

"After some discussion of launching another commando raid —a full-scale one this time," Groves wrote in *Now It Can Be Told,* "General Marshall, at my behest, proposed to [Field Marshal] Sir John Dill [of the Combined Policy Committee set up to supervise the joint efforts of the United States, the United Kingdom, and Canada] that, instead, the plant be made a first priority bombing objective."

From the start, Tronstad and Wilson had been vehemently opposed to an air bombardment of the Vemork plant, but this time neither of them nor the Norwegian government in exile was consulted. It was decided by the Combined Chiefs of Staff, "after careful consideration," according to the British account as recorded in *Norsk-Hydro,* published in Oslo in 1955, "that the objective was better suited to bombing than to sabotage. The British Government [has] received information from sources worthy of confidence to the effect that the Germans [have] strengthened their security to the point where it would be impossible to carry out sabotage operations. . . . In future they would have no success at all."

In view of the brilliant precision-bombing record established by the United States Army Air Force's daylight bombers in different war theaters, the Combined Chiefs chose the U.S.'s Eighth Air Force in Britain, under the command of General Ira C. Eaker, to execute the operation. After studying maps of the gorge cut by the Måne River, the mountains rising like walls on each side, and the snug, cliffside location of the plant, Eaker expressed no great confidence that the target could be destroyed by bombing. But by then, November 1943, America had made such advances toward constructing an atomic bomb that Groves wanted at all costs to prevent the Germans from making one first. In the end, the urgency, stakes, and logistics involved made a bombing attempt the inevitable choice.

When the bombers climbed into the air over Britain in the predawn hours on November 16, the weather was bad, with cloud banks as low as 500 feet and as high as 10,000 feet, serious icing conditions, and high turbulence. There were 460 aircraft altogether, Flying Fortresses and Liberators of the VIII Bomber Command, and they were all heavily loaded with the extra fuel needed for the return trip. To diffuse any possible retaliation by German fighters, it was to be a three-pronged attack. Two divisions were to attack targets near Stavanger and Oslo respectively. The third division, under the command of Major John M. Bennett, would concentrate on Vemork.

One by one, in rapid succession, they took off and climbed into the clouds and darkness, where they stacked up in circling layers, at predetermined altitudes, until they formed groups and squadrons for the flight across the North Sea. The Vemork plant was to be attacked between 11:30 A.M. and noon, when most of the workers would be at lunch, and the forecast for southern Norway during that time span called for clear skies, with clouds closing in shortly thereafter.

It was daylight when the third division, in standard box formations, headed out over the North Sea at 14,000 feet. German fighters were expected, but none were encountered. In fact, the flight across the sea was so uneventful that they reached the Norwegian coast, between Kristiansand and Stavanger, eighteen minutes ahead of time. Major Bennett, reluctant to strike the plant before the workers left for lunch, ordered the whole formation to turn back and circle over the sea for eighteen minutes. It was one of those command decisions that can haunt a man for years after a war is over. For when the Flying Fortresses turned and approached the Norwegian coast again, they were met by intense antiaircraft fire from alerted enemy defenses. One bomber was set afire, and another, forced out of its formation pattern with a blasted engine, started homeward. Ten men were seen parachuting from the flaming bomber into the sea as Bennett, in the command plane, led the way over a puzzling network of mountains, valleys, woods, and fjords toward the target.

The most precise navigation was required, and at 11:30 A.M. the bombardiers in the lead formation had the Vemork plant in their Norden sights. From an altitude of over two miles, the first pattern of bombs started downward. During the next thirty-three minutes, over 700 500-pound bombs fell in the deep valley where Norsk Hydro made its precious heavy water. They fell toward a target suddenly obscured by the emission of turbid smoke from the smoke generators erected by the Germans after the Gunnerside raid. This smoke made it difficult, if not impossible, to concentrate the attack on vital installations. The bombs fell everywhere, one scoring a direct hit on a newly built air-raid shelter; sixteen Norwegians were killed.

Four bombs struck the power plant, but they caused remarkably little damage to the machinery. Five houses and four troops huts were destroyed, and three other houses damaged. The penstocks were hit by three bombs, and the sluices on top of the mountain were struck by two. Only the automatic closing of the sluice gates prevented a flood disaster for those caught on the ledge of rock on which the plant stood. They were more than caught; they were completely cut off, for a direct hit collapsed the suspension bridge over the gorge, while another tore up the railroad tracks leading from the plant along the shelf of rock into Rjukan.

The prime target, the electrolysis plant where the heavy water was produced, received two hits. The four top floors were damaged, but the machinery was scarcely harmed, and, down in the basement, the heavy-water installations were not even touched.

Owing to an unfortunate error, fifteen of the bombers mistook the nitrate plant at Rjukan for the electrolysis plant at Vemork. They dropped over a hundred 250-pound bombs there, destroying the packing plant, the central workshop, and the installations for the concentration of acid. Water, gas, ammonia, and steam pipes were cut, sprinkler systems knocked out, and electrical wires destroyed. When workmen rushed to repair the broken ammonia pipes, the noxious fumes grew so strong that the charcoal and chemical filters in their gas masks proved to be useless. They had to use oxygen masks and keep going back for refills until the pipes were sealed.

Since the valley where Rjukan stands is only 300 yards wide, with the nitrate plant on one side and the town on the other, it was a miracle that no bombs fell on the town itself. Altogether, twenty-two people were killed during the Vemork-Rjukan air attack, including one man, on skis several miles away in the mountains, who was struck by splinters from a stray bomb dropped by one of the homebound aircraft.

In London, the Norwegian government in exile, informed of the reaction in Norway to the killing and the destruction, issued a strong protest to the British and American governments against the saturation air attack, which "was carried out without any advance notice being given to the Norwegian government . . . and seems out of all proportion to the objective sought."

The protest went on to say that "the Norwegian military authorities have always done everything possible to furnish the Allies with the most detailed and precise information on factories and installations in Norway, as well as information as to what use they were being put to by the enemy for war purposes." Referring to the Gunnerside operation and others like it, the protest said that the Norwegian military authorities "have on several occasions taken action to put factories and other industrial installations in Norway out of working order if their production was necessary to the enemy's war effort. . . . If the aim of this bombing was to stop the production . . . of heavy water, better results could have been achieved by specialized methods of attack than by over-all bombing of the factories. . . ."

But if the bombing destroyed neither the rebuilt high-concentration cells in the basement of the electrolysis building, nor the heavy water they contained, it did, in a roundabout way, achieve its objective. The Germans came to the realization that any attempt to resume production of heavy water at Vemork would be met by internal sabotage, another air bombardment, or another commando raid. They were convinced that the plant, the town, and the surrounding mountains were infested with undercover agents and commandos, even though not a single participant in the Gunnerside raid had been caught. As for another air bombardment, the Germans knew they did not have the fighter planes in southern Norway to intercept a powerful armada of Flying Fortresses. The only solution, from the German point of view, was to ship all of Vemork's heavy water, in all its different concentrations, to the relative safety of the German Reich.

It did not take long for Einar Skinnarland, who had taken over all radio duties on Hardanger Plateau following Knut Haugland's departure for Oslo, to be informed of these plans. His brother Torstein's brother-in-law, Gunnar Syverstad, made the heavy-water determinations in the plant's lab. Syverstad got in touch with Skinnarland, who in turn, by means of his radio station powered by a makeshift water wheel, made contact with London.

"It is of the utmost importance," London emphasized after hearing the news that the entire stock of heavy water was to be shipped to Germany, "to try to get all the different concentrates contaminated with oil without leaving evidence traceable to the source. This will seriously affect any start-up of production in Germany."

It was London's primary aim to prevent any of the heavy water, whether of high or low concentration, and whether contaminated or not, from reaching Germany. The contamination idea was merely a stopgap measure in the event an attempt to destroy the entire shipment of heavy water failed.

On February 3, Skinnarland reported that most of the low concentrates had been contaminated and that they were being transferred to barrels inside the plant in preparation for shipment to Germany. "Regarding preventing transport to Germany," he went on in the same message, "I do not at this time have details on the timing, nor is the mode of transport definite."

It was at about this time that Vemork's transport engineer, Kjell Nielsen, joined the conspiracy to prevent the Germans from carrying out their plan. He would know about any shipment of heavy water from the plant, since he would be making the arrangements for it. And he was an absolutely loyal Norwegian who could be trusted.

Recalling the first clandestine meeting he attended, Nielsen said, "One evening in the beginning of February, 1944, I was visiting some friends near the plant when the doorbell rang, and my host said somebody wanted to see me. Outside I met a fellow I had never seen before, but he asked me to come with him and meet someone whose identity had to be kept secret."

Nielsen walked cautiously around a dark corner of the house

with this man, who was Rolf Sörlie, one of Claus Helberg's contacts before the Gunnerside operation. Sörlie had earlier left his job at the Vemork plant and joined Einar Skinnarland and Knut Haukelid in the mountains. The "someone whose identity had to be kept secret" was none other than Haukelid, who since the Gunnerside operation had spent a full year in the open wastes of Hardanger Plateau. After he and Arne Kjelstrup had eluded the German troops searching the plateau the year before, Kjelstrup, ill and emaciated, had been ordered back to Britain. Haukelid, living a life of extreme deprivation and hardship, had carried on alone in trying to establish Milorg, the Military Organization of Resistance, in Telemark, to be ready for the eventual takeover of the country from the Germans.

"Haukelid was awful to look at," Nielsen remembers, "with a dense beard, and marked by the tough life in the mountains. The other fellow was Rolf Sörlie, who was called 'Finn.' They wanted to talk to me about some information they'd received about German plans to take away the remaining stock of heavy water from Vemork."

Since the first exchange between Skinnarland and London about the shipment of heavy water, there had been a continuous series of communications: from Syverstad to Skinnarland to London and back from London to Skinnarland; from Skinnarland to Haukelid and Sörlie; and now from Haukleid and Sörlie to Kjell Nielsen. Even if the Germans had succeeded in cutting off or intercepting one step in the series, the information would have continued flowing. More and more Norwegians were enlisting in the underground movement, some by quitting their jobs and forming brigades in the mountains, others by not seeing what they were not supposed to see or by remaining silent when silence was called for. The Germans knew the movement was attracting new recruits and gathering momentum, but they could do no more about it than they could limit the number of raindrops that fell on Rjukan when it rained.

"I offered my host some kind of explanation and left with Haukelid and Sörlie," Nielsen said. "The three of us went down the road to my room, situated on the first floor of a small building opposite the main guesthouse belonging to the company. There was an open staircase, with heaps of snow around the bottom steps. The place was well suited for secret meetings."

Haukelid and Sörlie wanted to know all the facts. Was it true that a transport was planned? How much heavy water was there? Would it be possible to destroy the lot? Nielsen confirmed that the remaining heavy water was being put in drums for shipment to Germany. The drums, marked "potash lye," were to be placed on railway cars at Vemork and taken by rail along the mountainside to Rjukan, and then to the rail-ferry at Mael. There they were to be put aboard the ferry, on the railway cars, and taken across Lake Tinn to Tinnoset at the far end, where they were to continue by rail to Heröya for transport by ship to Germany, probably Hamburg. A definite date for the shipment had not been decided.

"I remember well, we agreed to recommend 'no action' to London," Nielsen said. "I claimed it would probably be very difficult for the Germans to extract concentrated heavy water from these uneven concentrations. I said they could hardly have the equipment to do this. Another strong argument was the probability of rather serious reprisals from the Germans against the people at Rjukan. We agreed to meet again in my room two days later, when Haukelid and Finn had got an answer from London."

Skinnarland radioed London on February 16, relaying the doubts expressed at the meeting in Nielsen's room about whether destroying the heavy water would be worth the resulting reprisals. The reply from London came that same day:

"Case considered. Very urgent that heavy water be destroyed. Hope this can be done without too serious consequences. Send our best wishes for good luck in the work. Greetings."

It now became evident that a third man would be needed for

the operation. Only Haukelid and Skinnarland had been trained to work with explosives, and Skinnarland had to be kept free for radio communication. So while Haukelid put Sörlie through a quick course in how to handle the plastic explosives they planned to use, Skinnarland tried by means of the underground grapevine to find a third man. Almost immediately he was given the name of a Rjukan resident who had shown exceptional courage fighting the Germans in April of 1940. The man worked as a surveyor, Skinnarland was told, so he had a *Schein*, a pass, that allowed him to travel almost anywhere in the area.

"We were in desperate need of a third man for the sabotage," Sörlie said later, "and suddenly Skinnarland came across the man who was one hundred per cent right for the job. His name was Knut Lier-Hansen, a tough young fellow who did not know what nerves meant. Seldom have I seen anyone become so enthusiastic at the prospect of being involved in an action that might be dangerous. And with his connections in the most unlikely places, he became of great help to us the last days. Amongst other things, he provided the car we were to use."

They held secret meetings in various places rather than in the same place each time, and only those who were needed at any given meeting attended that meeting. Nielsen did not necessarily know about meetings that Lier-Hansen attended, nor did Lier-Hansen and Syverstad know about meetings to which they were not invited. Only Haukelid and Sörlie attended every meeting, and when everyone was present, only limited areas of discussion were touched upon. Lier-Hansen did not know at first, for example, what the plan was except that it was dangerous. It was only after he became a bona-fide member of the group that the objective of the sabotage was openly discussed.

There were four possible ways of achieving that objective. First, they could attempt to break into the plant and destroy the heavy water before the drums were loaded on the railway cars. But after the successful Gunnerside raid, the Germans had bricked up all the doors and windows on the ground and first floors. To enter the building now it was necessary to report to a guard on the ground level, then go up a staircase to the second floor and report to another guard standing by a steel door behind which other guards were stationed. Fifty heavily armed commandos might have succeeded in storming the building and destroying the heavy water inside, but three men would almost certainly be killed before they so much as reached the staircase leading to the second floor. If by some miracle they did succeed in getting inside the building, each drum of heavy water would have to be destroyed separately, and there were thirty-nine of them.

A second possibility was to blow up the heavy-water train while it was en route along the mountain ledge between Vemork and Rjukan. Norsk Hydro's dynamite shack, containing over two tons of dynamite, lay just alongside this two-and-a-half-mile stretch of track. If they could blow up the dynamite shack while the train was passing, the train would be blown off the ledge into the gorge below, the drums would burst open, and the heavy water would flow harmlessly onto the icy surface of the Måne River.

This seemed the simplest and surest plan, but there were disadvantages. For one thing, there was already one German soldier guarding the dynamite shack, and not even Kjell Nielsen, the plant's transportation engineer, could predict what security measures the Germans would take along the track once the shipment of heavy water started. If the Germans sent a scout train, for example, the resulting explosion would be meaningless and only make the Germans that much warier. An even greater drawback was the great loss of life such a derailment would entail, because it had become daily routine, since the destruction of the suspension bridge across the gorge, for Vemork's workers to use the railway to get to and from Rjukan. The Germans, if only to preclude any local sabotage attempt, would undoubtedly load the drums of heavy water onto one of these "workers" trains.

The third idea—to destroy the train with explosives after it had crossed Lake Tinn and was en route from Tinnoset to Heröya —presented even greater disadvantages insofar as the endangering of Norwegian lives was concerned. That route was much used by civilians throughout the year, and if the train's cargo included tanks of ammonia, as it usually did, probably no one would survive.

The prospects looked so dim that they discussed possibly recommending to London that the ship carrying the heavy water to Germany be sunk in the North Sea, by either submarine or aircraft. It was during this discussion that their imaginations turned back to that part of the journey where the rail-ferry would be crossing Lake Tinn. This led to a fourth plan, and the one they finally adopted—to sink the rail-ferry before it reached Tinnoset, at the far end. Lake Tinn's deepest point was almost a quarter of a mile. If they could place a charge below the ferry's water line, a charge that would explode while the ferry was crossing that point, the cargo would never be salvaged.

But, as with the rejected plans, there was the question of the loss of innocent lives. The ferry would go down with all aboard, including her Norwegian crew and passengers. No one, no matter how young, old, or important, could be warned on boarding the ferry, much less forewarned the day before. Everything must appear normal and routine right up to the moment the ferry reached the deepest part of the lake and the plastic charge exploded. The lake at that point was little more than a mile wide, so the explosion would have to have sufficient force to sink the ferry rapidly, before the crew had a chance to save lives—and the drums of heavy water, too—by beaching her.

This understandable reluctance to kill innocent Norwegians led to a message from Skinnarland to London in which official authorization was requested:

"We consider safest solution is to sink the ferry by civil sabotage on Tinnsjo [Lake Tinn] with all heavy-water barrels aboard. Can we be authorized to do this? Only other possibility is complete demolition by explosives of the entire train for example near Svelgfoss. We must expect reprisals in connection with action. Answer soonest."

The next day London wired back:

"Approve sinking of the ferry with heavy-water cargo in deep water, preferably between Hesleviken and Digerud. If bottom valves are opened, this must be combined with an explosion to indicate limpet attack from the outside. The engines must be put out of operation so the ferry cannot continue to shallow water. The sinking must not fail, because the attack methods will then become known. Leave behind British uniform items if possible at suitable place. Good luck."

After another meeting, at which Nielsen was able to provide the exact date and time (Sunday morning, February 20) of the heavy-water transport, Haukelid wasted no time in going directly to the ferry dock at Mael, dressed as a workman, to reconnoiter the target. There were three ferries plying Lake Tinn in 1944; by checking the timetables he learned that an old, screw-driven ferry, the *Hydro*, whose skipper was Captain Erling Sorensen, would be the one leaving Mael early on Sunday, February 20. He waited for the *Hydro* to pull into Mael, then boarded her as a passenger for the trip to Tinnoset, at the far end of the long, narrow lake. Checking his watch, he noted that it took the ferry about half an hour after leaving the dock at Mael to reach the really deep water, and that for a full twenty minutes after that she churned through water as deep as 1,300 feet. Thus if the charge could be detonated forty-five minutes after she left the dock at Mael, there would be just enough leeway for either a ten-minute delay in sailing or for an unusually speedy trip.

They already had the necessary explosives—the same adhesive, puttylike plastic that Rönneberg and Strömsheim had used on the high-concentration cells—but they could not use ordinary fuses this time, because the time delay was too long. They needed electric detonators, and an absolutely reliable timing device.

"Using alarm clocks was Sörlie's idea," Lier-Hansen said

later. "Old-fashioned, but he knew what he was talking about."

Sörlie had a friend, a retired Norsk Hydro inspector, John Dieseth, whose hobby was repairing old clocks and watches. Dieseth had a handicraft shop in town, with a little workshop, strewn with bits of metal, wire, springs, and the insides of old clocks, just above the shop on the first floor. When Sörlie visited him one night and explained the situation, Dieseth donated one of his own alarm clocks to the sabotage plan; Sörlie obtained the second from another friend in town. They made an odd couple, Dieseth in his late sixties, Sörlie in his early twenties, but they were both dedicated resistance men, closely linked by the pride they shared in the way Rjukan had opposed the German invasion in 1940.

The next night, Haukelid and Sörlie, using Dieseth's workshop as a base, prepared the plastic explosives while Dieseth worked on the two alarm clocks. It was Haukelid's plan to place the charge in the bows of the ferry, in accordance with London's instructions that she be prevented from moving to shallow water before sinking. If the explosion in the bows blew a hole in her metal skin, the stern would rise above the surface as forward compartments became flooded. Once the bows went under, the railway cars on deck, loaded with drums of heavy water, would roll forward with the tilt of the ferry and tumble into the lake. The drums would sink almost as fast as the railway cars themselves, since the heavy water was heavier than ordinary water. Moreover, even if the ferry's engines continued operating, the power they generated would be useless with the propeller and rudder out of the water.

To accomplish this, the hole would have to be big enough to start the ferry sinking almost immediately. Enough water would have to rush in to pull the stem down and send the stern up. But how big was big enough? They thought of the huge penstocks that feed the turbines at Vemork. Each one, with a diameter of a little over five feet, carries tons of water every minute down from the mountains, enough to sink any ship. Should they make the hole the same size—about five feet across? Haukelid calculated, using figures he had obtained on the *Hydro*'s tonnage and water displacement, and decided to make the hole a little smaller, to give the passengers a fighting chance to jump overboard and swim to shore.

Working together, Haukelid and Sörlie kneaded nineteen pounds of plastic explosive into a sausage twelve feet long—enough to make a hole about four feet across—and wrapped it in burlap for easier handling. They would insert the electric generators at the last minute, when they set the alarm clocks and wired everything together.

Meanwhile, Dieseth had removed the bell, but not the bell hammer, from each of the two alarm clocks. After determining the exact range and location of the hammer's swing, he attached, in place of the bell, an electric insulator from an old telephone receiver, a small piece of Bakelite, in the middle of which he affixed a metal contact with a wire running from it. When everything was correctly wired and the clocks were set, the bell hammer, once the "alarm" began to ring, should strike the metal contact, complete the electric circuit, and start the current flowing. This would immediately activate the percussion caps in the electric detonators, which in turn would set off the sausage-shaped bomb. Dieseth used four flashlight batteries to power the entire mechanism, and soldered the terminals to be certain the wires would not come loose.

Before dawn, Haukelid and Sörlie left the workshop with the equipment and climbed back up to their hut on the mountain ridge above the town. It took them three hours, as usual, and they were both ready for bed when they arrived. To be absolutely sure that the alarm clocks were reliable, they wired an electric detonator to each one and laid the detonators on some planks of wood. After setting the clocks to go off when it was time for them to get up that evening, they went to sleep.

Six hours later they sprang to their feet and grabbed guns at the sound of rifle fire—two sharp cracks in rapid succession. Sörlie pointed his Sten gun out the window, fully expecting to see German troops, while Haukelid stepped to the door with a Tommy gun cocked and ready. Suddenly they looked at each other, lowered their guns, and shook their heads in amusement. The two detonators had gone off on schedule, their percussion caps sounding almost exactly like rifle shots in the cold dry air. Old Dieseth had done his job well; the timing devices worked perfectly.

There was still the question of what each man involved in the sabotage would do if all went well and the ferry did indeed sink when and where it was supposed to. Knowing how effective the Gestapo was in obtaining information, they all wanted to avoid being questioned afterward. Gunnar Syverstad's plan was to leave the Vemork plant altogether and, like Rolf Sörlie, join the underground. Knut Lier-Hansen said that, barring some mishap, he would return to his surveyor's job on the Monday following the sabotage as though nothing had happened. Knut Haukelid, who deserved some civilized living after all he had been through, was to escape to Sweden and await further orders. Kjell Nielsen, the plant's transport engineer, was in perhaps the most precarious position, since he would naturally be pinpointed as the man who knew all about the shipment of heavy water from the plant. He, too, could escape to Sweden, but because London wanted a future contact between someone at the plant and Einar Skinnarland, he was asked if he could find some plausible reason for staying on despite his involvement.

"I had had some pain on my right side and suggested that I undergo an operation to have my appendix removed," Nielsen said later. "I called a sister in Oslo and arranged to have the operation on Saturday, February 19, the day before the action. This would give me the kind of alibi I needed to return to the plant afterward, though I was uneasy at the thought that I might start talking about the planned action while I was under anesthesia."

The final question was what to do about Vemork's chief engineer, Alf Larsen, who was in charge of the production of heavy water at the plant. "The chief engineer was not involved in the sabotage at all, but could be suspected," Nielsen said. "Haukelid decided this short and sweet. Larsen had to be taken away, and I was asked to tell him. He was my boss; we went to and from the plant in the same car and normally had our meals together. A couple of days before the action I told him that something was going to happen and that in his position he would be vulnerable. He therefore had to disappear; I told him where to meet Haukelid and the others on Saturday evening, in sports clothes and with very light hand luggage."

Sörlie put it another way. "Larsen was in charge of heavy-water production at Vemork," he said. "It was decided to send him to Sweden, so the Germans would have a scapegoat."

As the day of the heavy-water shipment approached, the Germans tightened their already strict security measures in anticipation of some sabotage attempt. An army detachment was sent to guard the railway line from Vemork to the ferry dock. Special SS troops began to appear at sensitive points all along the Rjukan valley. Two Fiesler Storch reconnaissance planes, using a landing strip not far from Vemork, scanned the surrounding mountains, lakes, and fjords from dawn to dusk. Under floodlights and the eyes of armed troops, the drums of heavy water, marked "potash lye," were loaded on railway cars at Vemork.

Haukelid and his men had to know with certainty when the transport was to start. They had to board the *Hydro* and lay their charges before the train arrived at Mael, but only after they were certain the train would arrive on schedule. Any breakdown in their intelligence reports, or any sudden change of schedule ordered by the Germans, would result not only in their sinking the wrong ferry, but also in the complete disclosure of their sabotage plans.

At another meeting, Nielsen confirmed the schedule and said that all thirty-nine drums of heavy water were already loaded on the railway cars. As an added check against a possible change in schedule, Lier-Hansen, using the special surveyor's pass that allowed him to go anywhere, talked with conductors and railway personnel. They all told him the same thing: the heavy-water transport was ready and would proceed as planned. The train would leave Vemork on Saturday and travel down to Rjukan, where it would be sidetracked until early Sunday morning, at which time it would move on to the dock at Mael, to be pushed by a small switch engine aboard the ferry for the trip to Tinnoset.

This would give Haukelid, Sörlie, and Lier-Hansen plenty of time on Saturday night, in the dark, while the *Hydro* was docked for the night at Mael, to board her and lay charges.

"I got hold of a car," Lier-Hansen said later, "driven by Olav Hansen of Rjukan. He used to drive me around on my different surveying jobs, so I told him I needed transport for some of my instruments. He swallowed my story and agreed to meet me and some friends of mine by his garage."

That evening, Saturday, February 19, Haukelid and Sörlie stole down from their mountain hut into Rjukan. The railway station had been closed to passenger traffic ever since the successful Gunnerside raid on the Vemork plant, but they could see, from a ledge overlooking the town, the two sidetracked flatcars loaded with the drums of heavy water. They were floodlighted and surrounded by armed German soldiers, a few of whom were actually sitting on the drums, apparently in response to General von Falkenhorst's earlier admonition to the guards at Vemork: "When you have a chest of jewels like this, you plant yourself on the lid with a weapon in your hand!" The soldiers appeared alert enough to be anticipating further orders, so there seemed no longer any reason to doubt that the two flatcars would be moved on to the ferry the next morning.

Haukelid and Sörlie hurried to join the others, in a back street in town, where the car was kept. Hansen, who was to drive the car, was there waiting for them with Lier-Hansen, and in a few minutes Larsen arrived, wearing the sports clothes suggested and carrying his most essential possessions in a small bag. Having been ordered by Haukelid, who represented the Norwegian government in exile, to leave his job and country and escape to Sweden, and being a loyal Norwegian, he looked upon this sudden departure as a grim necessity. As Jomar Brun's successor at the plant, though, he was well known in town, a respected citizen who would not be expected to take part in clandestine meetings. It was important, therefore, that they leave as soon as possible, but when Hansen pulled the choke and turned on the ignition, the car refused to start. They had managed to get some extra gasoline, so the trouble was not fuel. Nor was it the battery. Could some water in the fuel pump have frozen? Though all were good mechanics, it took them over an hour to get the car started.

"Olav drove us to within about three-quarters of a mile of the ferry dock at Mael, and I told him to wait there," Lier-Hansen recalled.

But Haukelid had changed his mind; he did not want Hansen to be involved in the sabotage, much less in the escape afterward.

"So I drove Olav back home to Rjukan and borrowed his car for the return trip," Lier-Hansen said. "I told him that it might take some time, as we had to travel to Tinnoset at the far end of the lake. He agreed, and when I got back to Mael, there was still plenty of time; it was a little before midnight. We parked the car a good way back from the ferry dock, in among some trees, and turned the headlights off."

There were no floodlights on at the station by the dock, and only an ordinary lamp on at the outboard end of the gangway.

They could see the blacked-out *Hydro* tied up at the dock, but no soldiers. It looked too easy, too simple. Could the Germans have set a trap? Lier-Hansen did not think so.

"I had done some reconnaissance at Mael earlier in the week," he said. "There were twenty to thirty German guards at the railway station by the ferry dock, but they were very careless. They played cards inside the station and hardly ever left the guardroom, people said. It sounded promising."

Haukelid handed Larsen a pistol and told him to wait by the car. If they were not back in two hours, or if he heard shooting, he was to drive off at once. He could leave the car at Kongsberg, take the train to Oslo, and from there find his own way to Sweden.

With Sten and Tommy guns, pistols, and hand grenades hidden beneath their parkas, Haukelid, Sörlie, and Lier-Hansen started toward the station. The cold night air had all the tree branches creaking in the wind, and on the road there was a thin, crackly layer of ice that seemed to monitor their every movement. When they came to a point on the hillside a few hundred yards away, Lier-Hansen, the only one with a pass that allowed him to go anywhere, went on ahead.

"If there were Germans about on the dock," he said later, "I was to let off a few rounds with my Tommy gun farther up the road in order to draw the Germans away from the ferry so the other two could get aboard with the explosives. I walked down to the station to take a look, and, right enough, the German soldiers were playing cards; some of them slept. I saw nobody outside."

Within minutes, Haukelid was leading the way across the dock onto the ferry. Like passengers intending to spend the night aboard after enjoying a few beers, they ambled forward, unchallenged by a single German guard, to a companionway leading from the deck to a passenger saloon below. On the way down they heard loud voices coming from the crew's quarters and crept closer to investigate.

"Almost the entire ship's crew was gathered together below at a long table, playing poker rather noisily," Haukelid wrote in his report to London. "Only the engineer and stoker were working, in the engine room, so there was no question of going in there."

Having already taken a trip aboard the *Hydro,* he led the way to a hatchway going from the passenger saloon down to the bilge. But before they could get the hatch open, they heard footsteps coming from the crew's quarters. Haukelid and Sörlie ducked behind some soft chairs in a corner of the saloon, while Lier-Hansen, counting heavily on his pass, held his ground with a casual air to avert suspicion and to cover for the others.

"It was a member of the crew," Lier-Hansen said, "John Berg, whom I knew from our athletic club. I was wearing a parka, so my Tommy gun was hidden from sight."

"You here, Knut?" Berg said.

"Yes, John," Lier-Hansen said. "With some friends," he quickly added as Haukelid and Sörlie stepped from their hiding place.

Berg looked puzzled and a little frightened. He did not know Haukelid or Sörlie, and the former appeared loaded down with something. The plastic explosive, twelve feet long, was looped like a huge sausage around his shoulders beneath his coat, his pockets were stuffed with clocks and hand grenades, and he was carrying a concealed Sten gun. But Lier-Hansen had been told by another crew member that Berg could be trusted.

"Hell, John," he said, "we're expecting a raid, and we have something to hide. It's as simple as that."

"Why didn't you say so?" Berg said. "No problem." He went over and pointed to the hatchway leading below decks. "This won't be the first time something's been hidden below."

As quickly and as quietly as possible, Haukelid and Sörlie slipped through the hatch and closed it behind them, leaving Lier-Hansen to chat with Berg and cover for them. Once below, they began to sweat and pant with excitement as they crawled forward on their hands and knees over the corrugated iron plates.

"We lifted one plate after another, but there was bilge water everywhere, which made it impossible to place this type of explosive," Sörlie said. "Reluctantly we began placing the charge fairly close to the passenger saloon, after crawling along the keel as far forward as possible. We had no other choice."

As they worked, the very sound of their breathing took on personality; they became aware of the wash of water in the bilges, of the ferry's slightest response to the wind hitting her super-structure. It was another thing to think of, a presage of what was going on above. Was Berg beginning to wonder what was taking them so long? They could have hidden ten things by now, in ten different places, but they still had not returned.

Working as fast and yet as carefully as possible, they taped the two alarm clocks and the batteries to the girders running fore and aft along the side of the ship, where the hull was dry and the tape would stick. Then Haukelid pressed the plastic, sausage-shaped charge against the ship's hull, in the form of a circle, and tied two detonator fuses—tubes filled with combustible matter—to each end of the circular charge. Taping these four fuses to-gether, he brought their loose ends to the clocks he had taped to the girders. He then set each clock to ring at 10:45 A.M., when the ferry should be over the deepest part of the lake, and wired electric detonators into the two-clock circuits. The most dangerous part of the operation came next, and there was the gnawing question of Berg and his possible impatience, or, worse, suspicion.

"They're still above in the saloon," Sörlie whispered. "Knut is talking his head off. It's all right."

A certain delicacy was required to set up a homemade timing device. Parts had to be connected and taped without undue em-phasis; wires, fuse ends, and battery terminals would break if the pressure brought to bear on them were angry or careless pressure.

With bated breath Haukelid cursed this crying need for industry in the black belly of a ship.

The bell hammer in each clock was separated from the "alarm bell"—or, rather, from the metal contact that had been inserted in the bell's place—by only one-third of an inch, so Haukelid was extremely careful not to jar the clocks in any way as he made the final connections. Telling Sörlie to hold the electric detonators well away from the fuses attached to the plastic bomb, he connected the batteries to the clocks. Nothing happened—which meant the circuits were still open. If all went well, the circuits would not close, and the bomb would not explode, until the "alarm" went off at 10:45 that morning, when they hoped, and expected, to be miles away. Haukelid completed the last and most dangerous step—connecting the electric detonators to the fuses. The bomb, fuses, detonators, clocks, and batteries were now all connected, and the clocks were ticking away.

They nodded—there was now just one-third of an inch between them and disaster—and quietly crawled aft over the corrugated iron plates to the ladder leading up to the passenger saloon. Though Berg did not ask them what had taken them so long, he was obviously relieved to see them. He had expected them to remain on board for the early-morning trip to Tinnoset, but they said they had to fetch some things. They'd be back, they said, in plenty of time before the ferry sailed.

"You on watch now?" they asked Berg.

"Yes, but I go off when the train arrives."

The three saboteurs smiled. "Lucky man."

Under the circumstances, it was a natural remark: Berg would soon be home, so he was lucky.

"I guess I am lucky," Berg said, laughing, "with guys like you about."

In recalling the incident, Lier-Hansen said, "We could now hear the train whistle, some distance from Mael, so Berg decided to go and get his gear. We waved good-by, went ashore, crossed a fence, and hurried up the hillside. It wasn't long before there were Germans everywhere."

The Germans had sat on their "chest of jewels"—the drums of heavy water—during the train ride from Vemork; they had thoroughly searched the train for explosives before the train's departure from Vemork. But they did not "sit" on the ferry, which was to carry their chest of jewels the full length of a lake a quarter of a mile deep. It was another case of German thoroughness outdoing itself.

Alf Larsen was waiting in the woods by the car, according to plan. He glanced at his watch when they rejoined him; it turned out that only three minutes of their two hours were left. They got in, with Lier-Hansen behind the wheel, and drove along the deserted road in the direction of Kongsberg. At Miland, after a ten-minute ride, Rolf Sörlie got out, took his skis from the rack on top of the car, and shook hands all around. He was going to join Einar Skinnarland up on Hardanger Plateau. As he started up the mountainside, he turned one last time and waved.

"I drove Haukelid and Larsen as far as Jondalen, which is about four kilometers from Kongsberg," Lier-Hansen said. "This would give them plenty of time to reach the Kongsberg railway station before the morning train left for Oslo. Then I drove back to Mael, parked the car in the same place, and walked into the woods above the ferry dock to wait until the ferry left. I wanted to be sure the heavy water was aboard."

While he waited, Haukelid and Larsen were boarding the morning train in Kongsberg for Oslo, and in a hospital in Oslo Kjell Nielsen was being wheeled into an operating room to have a perfectly healthy appendix removed. It was a crucial morning all around, for if Nielsen gave away the sabotage plan while under anesthesia, if he went so far as to name names, the bomb would be defused before the ferry sailed, and the hunt for the saboteurs would start. A telephone call from the hospital was all Germans needed.

At Mael, the intrepid Lier-Hansen, waiting in the woods, watched armed German guards being posted along the line of tracks from the station to the ferry. On orders from the officer in charge, the flatcars began moving forward, guarded in front, at the rear, and along both sides. The heavy water might have been nitroglycerin, they were so careful in getting the drums aboard the *Hydro*.

It was a little after ten o'clock when the ferry, with the flatcars lashed to her deck and with fifty-three people aboard, let go her mooring lines, churned away from the dock, and began cutting through the icy waters of Lake Tinn.

For Captain Sorensen it was the first trip of the day, a pleasant day at that, with the low morning sun sparkling through the trees along the shore. He had a brother who had twice been torpedoed in the frigid North Atlantic, where survival depended not upon swimming so much as upon getting into a lifeboat in time. Here in this landlocked lake, inaccessible even to a midget submarine, a captain could relax as though it were peacetime. That is what Sorensen was doing, relaxing on the bridge, when it happened.

The *Hydro* seemed to stop, or, rather, to contract for a moment, as though her entire structure were locked in combat with the sheer power of the explosion. Tremors ran upward and outward through her girders and ribwork. She shook and faltered as water surged through her blasted hull, and she began to list to her port side.

"About 10:30 I was on the bridge when I heard an explosion down in the belly of the ship," Sorensen said later. "I understood right away what it was—a bomb.

"The ship keeled over to the port side, and after a few minutes she was lying flat. I could walk on the ship's starboard side, which was still above water, as though it were a floor. I got my coat off, but forgot to remove my boots. So when she started to go down I jumped into the water and swam about fifteen feet from the ship. By then the stern was very high and the propeller was still turning. Then she went down, bow first, in the deepest part of the lake."

The flatcars broke loose before she disappeared from sight and, carrying the drums of heavy water with them, rolled off the deck into the lake. Haukelid's estimate of the time it would take the ferry to sink was off by only one minute. It took four minutes instead of the five he had predicted, and in that time twenty-seven people on board were able to jump into the water. These twenty-seven included four German servicemen, and they were all saved. The remaining twenty-six, including women and children, went down with the ship, into rock-ribbed chasms too deep for divers ever to reach. Debris, life belts, oars, chairs, and lifeboats were scattered about on the water, and in time four of the drums, half filled with heavy water of low concentration, bobbed to the surface. They were of little use to Germany now, but of great use to the survivors, who held on to them until members of the crew climbed into a lifeboat and came and picked them up.

Kjell Nielsen's fears that he would talk under anesthesia were unfounded.

"Nothing happened," he said, "and Sunday afternoon I heard that the ferry had sunk, unfortunately with many victims. The nurse in charge of my room happened to be from Rjukan, and she was able to tell me a great deal.

"On Monday the Germans called the hospital, and it was confirmed that I had been operated on for appendicitis. I was never questioned by anybody. . . ."

That same Monday, Rolf Sörlie, after "a strenuous trip on skis across the mountains," joined Einar Skinnarland up on Hardanger Plateau. Lier-Hansen returned to work in Rjukan as usual. The sinking of the *Hydro* made headlines in town—RAILWAY FERRY "HYDRO" SUNK IN THE TINNSJO—but no one suspected Lier-Hansen of having anything to do with it.

In Oslo, Haukelid and Larsen bought a Monday-evening newspaper to read the same news, only in smaller print. Sabotage was increasing throughout Norway to the point where the Germans were doing their best to suppress the reporting of it. Haukelid, who was later to receive one of Britain's highest honors, the Distinguished Service Order, for the part he played in the sinking of the ferry, succeeded in reaching Stockholm with Larsen. Once there, the lighted streets, the unabashedly glaring headlights, the shopwindows full of things to buy, and the restaurants lavish with tablecloths, wine, and varied menus, surprised and delighted them. After a few days, Larsen boarded a plane for Britain; Haukelid remained behind, to enjoy the pleasures of an open, unblacked-out city for a few weeks before returning to his comrades in the mountains of Norway.

This ended all German attempts to obtain heavy water from Norway, and destroyed any hopes German scientists may have entertained of constructing an atomic bomb. As German scientist Dr. Kurt Diebner, put it after the war:

"When one considers that right up to the end of the war, in 1945, there was virtually no increase in our heavy-water stocks in Germany, and that for the last experiments early in 1945 there were in fact only two and a half tons of heavy water available, it will be seen that it was the elimination of German heavy-water production in Norway that was the main factor in our failure to achieve a self-sustaining atomic reactor before the war ended."

Ironically, the men most actively involved in all the sabotage, those who risked their lives under poor survival conditions to prevent the heavy water from reaching Germany, did not realize what they had accomplished until the war was virtually over.

Colonel John Wilson, in his official SOE report after the war about the sinking of the *Hydro,* put it this way:

"It was nearly eighteen months before even many of those who had taken part in the various actions realized to the full the great value of the work they had done. There were many service officers who disparaged the whole business. To those in the know, however, and they were very, very few, it was a most anxious time. It is interesting to note in the file of papers, always kept in a safe, a paper written on 10th August, 1943, which prophesied, 'From the information available it appears that it will take two years before the results of [these nuclear experiments] are brought into actual military operation.' The estimate was not far out, as the first atomic bomb was dropped on Japan on 6th August, 1945."

When the British Prime Minister, Winston Churchill, read in a Special Forces report of the great contribution made by these dedicated Norwegians, he wrote across the front page: "What is being done for these brave men in the way of decorations?"

Every member of the Gunnerside operation received both British and Norwegian military decorations after the war. Their story of survival, sabotage, and escape has become one of the proudest chapters in Norway's proud history.

INDEX